A fundamental step forward in the evolution of Gisèle Chaboudez's reflection on sex and gender, *What Can We Know About Sex?* is an impeccable and thorough analysis of one of the most hotly debated issues today. It corrects many misunderstandings, and is precise, explicative and novel. Chaboudez provides a rigorous reading of Lacan's work, following his articulations step by step, and demonstrating how, for psychoanalysis, there cannot be any sexual norm. Her reflection on Lacan's notion of the feminine enhances the radically new perspective and the subversion inherent in an idea that is not yet fully appreciated in its individual and social consequences.

Dr Paola Mieli, *President,*
Après-Coup Psychoanalytic Association, New York

What Can We Know About Sex?

Despite the progress made by psychoanalysis since Freud's discovery of the sexual nature of the unconscious, analysts have tended to explore psychical causality independently of the role of the biological factors at play in sexuality. *What Can We Know About Sex?* explains how Lacan's work allows us to make new links between the sexual laws of discourse, gender and what Freud called the 'biological rock' in human life, allowing a new perspective not only on the history of the sexual couple but on contemporary developments of sexuality in the 21st century. Gisèle Chaboudez's insights demonstrate that the old phallic logic that has been so dominant is now in the process of being dismantled, opening up the question of how people can relate sexually and what forms of jouissance are at stake for contemporary subjectivity.

What Can We Know About Sex? will be a key text for analysts, academics and students of feminism, gender and sexuality.

Gisèle Chaboudez, a medical doctor and psychiatrist, trained with Jacques Lacan until 1981, and is now a psychoanalyst in private practice in Paris. Author of several acclaimed books, she is Vice President of the Espace Analytique group and editor of the journal *Figures de la Psychanalyse*.

The Centre for Freudian Analysis and Research Library

Series Editors: Anouchka Grose, Darian Leader, Alan Rowan

CFAR was founded in 1985 with the aim of developing Freudian and Lacanian psychoanalysis in the UK. Lacan's rereading and rethinking of Freud had been neglected in the Anglophone world, despite its important implications for the theory and practice of psychoanalysis. Today, this situation is changing, with a lively culture of training groups, seminars, conferences, and publications.

CFAR offers both introductory and advanced courses in psychoanalysis, as well as a clinical training programme in Lacanian psychoanalysis. It can provide access to Lacanian psychoanalysts working in the UK and has links with Lacanian groups across the world. The CFAR Library aims to make classic Lacanian texts available in English for the first time, as well as publishing original research in the Lacanian field.

The Baby and the Drive
Lacanian Work with Newborns and Infants
Marie Couvert

Treating Autism Today
Lacanian Perspectives
Edited by Laura Tarsia and Kristina Valendinova

Critique of Psychoanalytic Reason
Studies in Lacanian Theory and Practice
Dany Nobus

What Can We Know About Sex?
A Lacanian Study of Sex and Gender
Gisèle Chaboudez

www.cfar.org.uk
www.routledge.com/The-Centre-for-Freudian-Analysis-and-Research-Library/book-series/KARNACCFARL

What Can We Know About Sex?

A Lacanian Study of Sex and Gender

Gisèle Chaboudez
Translated by Lindsay Watson

Routledge
Taylor & Francis Group

LONDON AND NEW YORK

Designed cover image: Rachel Kneebone, Bewitching Balls Triptych, 2011, Porcelain, 14 3/16 x 27 15/16 x 9 1/4 in. (36 x 71 x 23.5 cm) © Rachel Kneebone. Photo © Stephen White Courtesy White Cube

First published 2023
by Routledge
4 Park Square, Milton Park, Abingdon, Oxon OX14 4RN

and by Routledge
605 Third Avenue, New York, NY 10158

Routledge is an imprint of the Taylor & Francis Group, an informa business

British Library Cataloguing-in-Publication Data
A catalogue record for this book is available from the British Library

ISBN: 978-1-032-25991-8 (hbk)
ISBN: 978-1-032-25990-1 (pbk)
ISBN: 978-1-003-28598-4 (ebk)

DOI: 10.4324/9781003285984

Typeset in Times New Roman
by Apex CoVantage, LLC

Contents

Translator's note

Translating Lacanian work is never straightforward, and some decisions made this time may differ from other time-honoured traditions of Lacanian or other translation, as well as the editorial decisions of publishers.

The terms 'sexual relation' and 'rock' of castration, as well as the 'one', the 'two', the 'all', sometimes have quotation marks in the text, in the former cases to distinguish them from ordinary usage, and in the latter two to facilitate comprehension. The more conventional editorial decision would be to use inverted commas only the first time each expression occurs.

I have taken a flexible attitude (now broadly sanctioned) with personal pronouns, especially in the case of the 'subject' (they, them, themself) or 'the baby', 'the infant' (it); sometimes the text refers to the old simple dichotomy between man and woman, him and her, and in those cases I have retained the old pronouns. It is hugely liberating not to have to use the clunky and distracting 'him-/herself' or 's/he', and makes for much smoother reading. Don't judge me too harshly if I have erred in some cases; no offence is intended, to gender, to sexuality or to semantics.

I have used 'phantasy' rather than 'fantasy' throughout, as in certain quarters it is deemed to refer to formations of the unconscious rather than creations of the imagination, and I like that differentiation.

Concerning the extraction of Adam's rib to form his object Eve, I have segued from 'extraction' (anatomical) to 'subtraction' (mathematical) as the context dictated.

Where the French *suppléance* occurs, I have sometimes followed Joan Copjec in reviving the ancient term 'suppleance' in English; at other times I have paraphrased using words such as 'supplementary', 'extra'.

It has been a pleasure as well as a challenge to translate Dr. Gisèle Chaboudez's rigorous analysis of the psychoanalytic conceptions and logics underlying the changes, psychical, societal and legal, that some of us are of an age to have lived through pretty much in their entirety, without necessarily taking cognizance of them and their full implications as they unfolded. They have radically transformed the geography of the sexual, emotional and legal lives of those of us who live in many of the contemporary civilisations of the Western world: granting us new freedoms, such as marrying or forming civil partnerships with anyone apart from close kin or the under-aged, regardless of sex or gender, while presenting us with vast and sometimes overwhelming responsibilities in the choices we can now make in how to knot together a 'sexual relation'. I am grateful to her for putting it all into a thorough, logical formulation and hope I have done justice to her work, so that others may benefit from her clear-sighted account of the disruption of time-honoured laws and systems that have now been thoroughly subverted. Or have they? . . .

Lindsay Watson
October 2021

Introduction

At the beginning of the last century, psychoanalysis discovered a new kind of knowledge about sex, contributing to the massive developments that have been observed in the field since then. In turn, these developments have to some extent drawn back the veil that once covered sexual structures. New facts have emerged that were quite unknown at the time of the earliest psychoanalytic discoveries, and these now call for interpretation. So, for example, the effects of the prohibition of incest on unconscious subjectivity – which were termed the Oedipus complex – no longer suffice to account for the gap that has been revealed in the relation between man and woman, as well as in their sexual relations, even if they play a significant role. In our societies where Christian faith has gone into decline, and where the law regulating the relation between the sexes has been called into question, the union of man and woman has proved to involve a gap which these institutions merely masked. What, then, does psychoanalysis make of these developments to which it has in itself contributed? Is it unsettled by the effects of the lifting of prohibition, to which it contributed by describing a repression that vastly exceeded the fundamental prohibition of incest? What does it have to say about the returns of the repressed that occurred after it had pointed out those very repressions? What can we know about sex when its time-honoured structures are being deconstructed?

It is not possible to speak in the name of psychoanalysis in its entirety, because in order to perceive a fundamental principle of the unconscious in addition to the one that Freud discovered and named Oedipus, you have to position yourself at a certain point and look in a certain way. Various facts and texts have to be deciphered, and we must recognise that the 'two' of sex is lacking in the structures of language. The psychoanalytic discourse arose out of this gap, which is present in the particular as well as the universal, and from that point onwards has expressed it in its own Freudian and Lacanian language. Still, the enigma of the absence of the 'two' of sex in the universe of discourse remains omnipresent.

Since Freud brought to light this knowledge about sex, a considerable distance has been travelled. What emerged was a kind of 'you are allowed to know' in a domain that had been marked for so long by repression and secrecy, even if for that very reason it was the subject of an obsession, and in that sense closer to the

DOI: 10.4324/9781003285984-1

mysteries of antiquity than to the confessional of Christianity, to which some have compared it. It gave rise to psychoanalytic thinking and scientific research, and fed into a number of human sciences and therapeutic practices. An inventory was made of the immensely broad field of symbolic constructions of the sexual, both in the history of civilisations and in subjectivity, and the psychical causality that was discovered in this way covered vast domains.

One might be excused for feeling that psychoanalysis had thus discarded ideas of the possible effect of biological factors in sexuality, assuming that they constituted an alien domain, outside of its field, without any relation to its object. And yet Freud never totally rejected the hypothesis of a biological 'rock', as he put it, which would explain why castration anxiety is so massively operative in every dimension of psychical life; and to the very end, he maintained that there was still a discovery waiting to be made here. Many of his followers ignored this idea, taking it to be a purely formal precaution to remind us that we actually have a body, and that it is not simply thought or represented, but also obeys biological laws. However, Freud's idea was absolutely serious and utterly realistic.

It is still not widely known that Lacan, in France, took up this idea. It was he who endeavoured to describe what characterised the sexual relation between man and women from a biological point of view, and evaluated its psychical effects. And the conclusion he reached, taking cognisance of the findings of nascent sexology, yet still quite distinct from them, led him to deduce a host of consequences for psychical life which had never before been noticed.

He invented a new object to describe the way in which certain particularities of the body were, and still are, borrowed in order to construct logics of desire; he added this to the Freudian concept of drive, which described the impact of speech on the body. From then on, the way was open for us to identify what it was that had been borrowed and assembled from the biological dimension of the sexual relation, to provide a basis for the logics of the unconscious that can be deciphered in religious myths, in cultural traditions and in everybody's dreams. The incidence of language on the body was already well recognised in psychoanalysis, and now it could be complemented by the incidence, which till then had remained unrecognised, of certain specific bodily facts on the institutions of language.

The unconscious effects on sexuality of the prohibition of incest have by now been comprehensively explored. On the other hand, it is important to explore precisely the ways in which certain traits may be borrowed from biology, and the impact they may have on psychical life and the institutions of language, in particular the sexual laws which regulate the social relations of men and women. Certainly this has nothing to do with the description of any biological substrate that might be used to justify those laws, as was proposed by the discourse of religion, but rather with the material upon which the cut of interpretation has operated, and the manner in which this cut has occurred. Deconstructing this structure is one thing; it is quite another to know under what conditions it was constructed, and in relation to which question.

These two facets of the incidence of language on sex, and that of sex on language, are not alternatives, they are not in mutual opposition; the two are constantly being superimposed on each other, and converge in the structuration of subjective experience. You do not need a laboratory to observe what it is that corresponds to Freud's hypothesis of a biological 'rock', in order to account for castration anxiety. It goes without saying that it is the most obvious constant factor in the sexual relation, and yet it is not explored in any scientific description, even though there are countless subjective examples. In order to make an interpretation of this on the basis of the Lacanian development of Freud's theory, it has been necessary to put together the widely dispersed fragments from the various stages of his thinking, and to reconstitute from these an overall logic in order to be able to appreciate its scope, while in parallel exploring its validity and its extension through clinical experience. In 2004, the publication of my book *Rapport sexuel et rapport des sexes* began an exploration of this, and showed how Lacan's response to one of Freud's last questions opened up a whole new field of psychoanalytic thinking.[1] Psychoanalytic practice seems to be the same, whether or not you consider sexuality strictly from the point of view of psychical causality, because the only means of intervention is speech. However, we can see that it is essential to take into account the interaction of the body with the structures of language as well as those of language with the body, because they work together to influence the way we conceive of psychical causality, as well as the way we intervene clinically.

***

Since time immemorial, the social relation of man and woman has been determined by civilisations according to an almost universal sexual law consisting of what nowadays is called the hierarchy of the sexes. Once psychoanalysis had described it based on the modes of symbolisation of sex by the unconscious, this law began to develop and change, leading to a broad reshaping of sexual roles in our society. And at the forefront of this development was the sexuality of the 'civilised couple'; indeed, the picture Freud painted of it was grim, attributing its grimness only partially to sexual repression, which at the time was very much at play and accompanied by numerous discourses on sex. Freud brought to our attention just how much human sexuality was marked by the prohibition of incest, which, in order to bring about the construction of the subject, separated love from sexuality in the earliest familial relations, to the extent that it became hard to reunite them in adulthood. The prohibition of incest also extended far beyond its legitimate field, and sexual repression found support in the prohibition in order to justify its own prohibitions so that all jouissance became incestuous, and therefore forbidden.

Freud had identified the major role of the phallus, and its correlative castration anxiety, in the construction of the subject of the unconscious that was established in infancy, where the difference between the sexes was understood on the basis of having a penis or being castrated. He recognised only a single libido, that of the phallus, which he considered at that time to be purely masculine, before eventually describing it as asexual. The unconscious at work in the structures of civilisation had retained only the phallic to symbolise sex, and had attributed it to the man by conflating it with the penis, according to the same phallic dialectic that was operative in childhood. From then on, it was taken as a given that there was an absence of a 'two' in sexuation according to the institutions of language, since there was only a single symbol serving as a reference for both sexes.

To this we can add Lacan's observation that the sexual law itself, which defines the social relations of sex, is also based on this phallic dialectic. The woman is represented as being deprived of the phallus in order to be able to *be* the phallus as object of desire, something which has now been put in question. The sexual law used the same phallic dialectic at that of infancy, completing it with an equivalence between woman and phallus in order to form this relation with the man as the one who has it. Lacan described this relation according to the law as 'a simplistic fiction, seriously in need of revision'.[2] He showed that it had been inaugurated by the metaphor from Genesis, where a rib was taken from Adam in order to create Eve, and where for a man union can take place only with a part of himself that has been restored to him having first been extracted from him.[3] This powerful and effective metaphor brought into being one sex based on the one who *has*, and the other on the one who *is*, a more or less timeless model of the symbolic relation of man with woman, linking the two sexes according to a simple grammar of complementarity between a subject and its object.

This law has been profoundly reshaped during the current phase of development and change of the social link between the sexes. It is now recognised as a fiction, far from being the natural basis of the relation between the sexes which it had claimed to be since time immemorial; it is now nothing but a single point of reference among others for the imaginary dimension of the sexual relation. It represents the grammar of discourse which the unconscious created at one stage, but no longer represents the universal and unique law of the relation between the sexes.

It has become apparent that the relation that had been declared complementary according to the law, between a subject of one sex and an object of the other, did not truly involve two sexes. It is merely the phantasy of one sex about the other, an autoerotic phantasy in which the subject is linked with an object considered to be its bodily complement, which leaves the desire of the other sex outside discourse. The relation prescribed by this law cannot be said to be sexual in the strict sense, which would involve two sexes,[4] but it can be said to be sexuated. Because it only inscribes one of the two sexes in discourse as the subject of speech, it divides[5] the articulation of the two sexes at its centre. The modalities of the sexual act are subjected to its influence, whether the parties in question subscribe to it or not.

In the middle of the last century, with the emergence of sexology, public discourses were filled with the growing awareness of a disjunction at the heart of the sexual act. A common difficulty was for a woman to achieve orgasm, and this was, with good reason, attributed to an ideology that excluded the very idea of her jouissance; and a great deal of effort went into combatting this. Patriarchal societies, especially those in the Christian tradition, established an ideology that amounts to a denial of feminine sexuality, which has been adopted to varying degrees in popular discourse in different epochs. Freud emphasised that a man's libido could only peak with a woman who gave up her own. However, certain religions of the ancient world approached this rather differently, suggesting that there was something else involved here too. The Eastern 'wisdom' that extolled certain behaviours with the aim of uniting the jouissances of the two sexes implied in so doing the fact that there was a difficulty in this conjunction, regardless of the intervention of monotheism, Christian or otherwise.

Lacan set about describing precisely what appeared to him to be a non-conjunction, revealing the biological 'rock', conjectured by Freud[6] to be at the root of castration anxiety. And he came to consider origin story of Genesis as a metaphorical representation of this 'rock', restoring the injunction to the One God. The extraction/subtraction of a rib from Adam in order to form his feminine partner, which is at the very heart of our sexual law, could be deciphered as a metaphor that substitutes this law for sexual conjunction, which is problematic by nature. Thus the God who authorised the extraction of the rib became the agent who had command over the 'rock' as well as over its solution.

In psychoanalysis, then, a pathway was opened up for a new conception involving a complex interaction between the body and psychical life that occurs in both directions, at different points. The 'sexual relation' of the man and the woman, including both their copulation and their social relations, had now to be considered from a dual perspective: on the one hand from the point of view of what is prescribed by sexual law, with the effects this has on each and every subject, and on the other hand from the point of view that this very law, in order to constitute itself, interpreted the biology of the sexual relation in a specific way.

For a long time in the psychoanalytic field the phallus was considered simply as a symbolic representation of the penis, which one either has or does not have, a narcissistic idea of castration; only recently has psychoanalysis taken into account the subjective functioning, based on biology, of the instrument of sexual jouissance, which is the real side of castration. This is doubtless because for a very long time psychoanalysis continued to orientate itself according to the Oedipal myth, and so conceived of this symbol as a child does, as an organ which is represented by the anguishing possibility of its absence. And in the same way, as long as civilised societies remained organised entirely according to the religious structures ordered around the Name of the Father, they were also, in this sense, Oedipal.

The phallic symbol is constructed on this biological 'rock' at play in the sexual relation, and not according to the presence or absence of the penis. And it is the attribute of a subject who speaks up, in what we call a phallic jouissance, because this subject is linked to the element that symbolises the desire of the mother. The recent developments of the social link between the sexes have recognised that women also have a subjective phallic jouissance, and have revised the scope of the sexual law which attributed 'having' to the masculine side and 'being' to the feminine. Henceforth, the phallic function is distributed differently, and is no longer imposed in a universal way. Currently it operates within a framework in which each subject authorises themself with respect to their sexuation and mode of jouissance only with reference to themself and a few others. Now that the universal relation has been deemed non-sexual, it remains for each individual to construct a sexual relation without universals.

This development, which has occurred concomitantly with the disappearance of sexual prohibition, has broadly re-shaped modes of sexuality, and has brought about the disappearance of certain sexual difficulties that could be imputed to the effects of prohibition and a universal law. A number of neuroses that were observed at the beginning of the last century have become less widespread and less acute, while certain other pathologies have disappeared altogether. Where jouissance can be achieved only through defying some prohibition, the entire field of love is affected by this, and the question is whether or not to go beyond the prohibition, rather than to know what love is. When the law's prohibition disappears, even if an unconscious prohibition persists, semblances collapse, functions are freed up and redistributed; and then the question arises as to what the sexual act consists in. And what is revealed is that the impasses that were masked by the old prohibition remain, intact.

This disappearance of prohibition from discourse has given rise to a number of concerns, including fears of the advent of an era of unlimited jouissance, or even of social perversion. This is based on the supposition that it was only prohibition that limited jouissance, whereas psychoanalytic experience has shown that it is limited by quite another barrier, a real one. Once prohibition disappeared, the thing that it was masking and which constituted the obstacle to the 'sexual relation' in another way was uncovered. The lifting of prohibition has not, indeed, resulted in unlimited jouissances; it is more a case of the unveiling of points of impossibility that it had previously masked, concerning the articulation of the two sexes in discourse. There is no reason here, however, to deny that the prohibition did exist, otherwise we could find ourselves in a considerable muddle.

In the various discourses and laws, since time immemorial, a single jouissance has been privileged: the phallic jouissance of the man, with its limit and its object. Articulating one jouissance with another is something different from conjoining just one jouissance with its object. And the jouissances of man and woman could never be simply conjoined, because they are in a profoundly asymmetrical relation. Each sex has a relation to the phallus, but this does not suffice to create a relation between them. Although it is expected to be a mediator, the phallus as major signifier of the sexual law does not articulate their jouissances in the sexual act any more than in their discourse. So this is what appears when the prohibition is undone, when the scene from Genesis, and its God, are no longer the objects of widespread belief.

Today's discourses remain void of any articulation of the two sexes with each other; the sexual law no longer reigns, but nonetheless it remains a reference, and henceforth it is only the particularity of each sexual couple that decides on their modes of jouissance. It remains organised according to phallic having and being, even though it is now distributed according to the unconscious desire of each individual and their relation to the other, rather than to a universal law. The woman is no longer considered lacking sexual feeling, nor is the man deemed to be split between love without desire, and desire without love. Feminine jouissance is widely referred to in discourse, as are the sexologists who have taken it upon themselves to spell out the ways in which orgasm can be achieved, while psychoanalysis has approached it via its subjective conditions. The symbolic order still does not inscribe the duality of sex – only the singularity of the subject and their object – but it is quite clear that this is not the whole story of jouissance, covering only its phallic dimension. Since the loosening of the stranglehold of the old sexual law, it seems easier to allow the articulation of two jouissances within a couple, on a case-by-case basis, without there being a discourse to articulate it, any more than there was before. There is still no sexual relation that can inscribe itself, either in the unconscious or in discourse, because it does not inscribe itself when it is sexual, involving two jouissances, and it is not sexual when it inscribes itself, since it concerns only one of them.

Little by little it has become clear that the sexual law, which was established as a symbolic relation between man and woman, is the logic that civilisation substituted for a defect in their biological conjunction. For a very long time this cut established a radical disjunction between the two sexes, along with their hierarchical exile. This is how Lacan put it: 'This is the reason why it has gone so badly since that time, regarding what actually goes on with this perfection that could be imagined as being the conjunction of two jouissances'.[7]

At the moment when this construction comes undone as a universal law, what becomes of the possible conjunction of two jouissances, of two sexes? What happens to the relation of man and woman at the moment when this sexual law shows itself to be a fiction, when nothing of what it laid down seems to be natural or necessary any longer? Where its complementarity between having and being proves not to form a relation of two sexes, but rather that of one sex in two bodies? Do man and woman then become equivalents in this domain, as they have become in others, knowing that equivalence does not form a relation? Is this relation reversed when there is no longer anything to prohibit it?

Access to a relation that could construct the duality of sex is indeed far from straightforward, and while current developments have removed a number of obstacles from it, it is still uncertain whether they suffice to open up a pathway to such a relation.

***

Several observations have since emerged to confirm and extend this deciphering, this interpretation of a thesis that remained latent in Lacan's thinking. Some questions which formerly remained unanswered have been resolved and allowed a further clarification. So now, we will take up this research in a new way, simplify the logic inherent in it, and refine it by integrating these new findings.

We can see ever more clearly that the time-honoured elaboration of the difference of the sexes, which created a hierarchy of their relation, still awaits a satisfactory interpretation. While a number of theories have been put forward, they have still not been sufficient to explain it decisively. In our civilisation today, this mode of differentiation is becoming blurred in the Western world, without anyone being able to give an adequate explanation for why this is so.

The psychoanalytic interpretation of the phallic phase of infancy proved inadequate to explain it, since it involved a logic of the phallus conflated with the penis. A further interpretation needs to be added to this, integrating the real of the sexual relation with what was excluded from it in order to establish the law.

Some have feared that this was a way of reintroducing biology into psychoanalytic thinking, which had differentiated itself from biology from the very beginning. But being differentiated from biology does not mean failing to recognise its scope, and it is worth identifying how culture dealt historically with certain biological facts, and how they were expressed in language in order to prepare the basis for the sexual laws that are comparable across various civilisations. It had effects on the articulation of the relation between the sexes, eliding one sex in its jouissance, and substituting a relation of subject to object for the relation that failed at the level of their jouissances. This cutting constituted the grammar of discourse, and its immense effects can be traced right from the roots of the logos up to the discourse of science, via the specific effects of the Middle Ages.

Since it has become apparent in our time that phallic jouissance, that of the subject of speech, is as much the domain of women as of men in all registers of society, the dividing lines between masculinity and femininity have been displaced. Masculinity is constructed entirely on phallic jouissance, while femininity adds another jouissance in the register of love. Structures based on the elision of the other sex as subject, so as to create a certain grammar of discourse, have reached their term. But now they have revealed the very stumbling blocks to which they were designed to provide a solution. Christianity's Name of the Father proved to be an extremely powerful symbolic agency where these constructions were concerned. If the need for the Name of the Father is no longer so obvious, it is only on condition that its old functions can be accessed in some other way.

Our aim here, then, is to explore these themes in a simplified and up-to-date fashion. Once we have studied the logic of the sexual law that was universally in force in the relation between the sexes up until the last century – constructed on the phantasy of one sex in the place of the other – we will examine the facts of the sexual relation of man and woman. We will then explore how these biological facts are interpreted by the law, eliding feminine jouissance. Following that, we will examine the causes of the extension of the prohibition of incest that accompanied this law, and the sexual substructure of the symbolic order that was constructed in this way. And all this will lead us, finally, to consider how current developments are causing a redistribution of jouissances.

Notes

1 Gisèle Chaboudez, *Rapport sexuel et rapport des sexes*, Paris, Denoël, 2004.
2 Jacques Lacan, *Logic of the Phantasy*, seminar of 19 April 1967.
3 Jacques Lacan, *Logic of the Phantasy*, seminar of 21 February 1968.
4 The word 'sexual' has been used in this sense in this context, but certainly not without recognizing that in another sense, 'sexual' does not necessarily imply two sexes, but rather whatever concerns sex in some way.
5 The common Latin etymology of *sexus* and *secare*, to cut, to divide, is well known. Another link is also sometimes mentioned with *sequi*, to accompany. The singular fate of the word 'sex' in our language is first of all to signify a sexuated set, feminine or masculine, then just one of the two, the feminine, and then in the 19th century extended to signify sexuality, and then (in the French language) the genitals of each sex, and then in our time, the sexual act. It has thus run the entire gamut of the sexual sphere, signifying successively and exclusively each of its parts, in order today to designate it in its entirety.
6 Jacques Lacan, *Anxiety, The Seminar Book 10*, ed. J-A Miller, Cambridge, Polity, 2014, pp. 238–9.
7 This is why we used the above quotation as the epigraph to *Rapport sexuel et rapport des sexes*; it sums up the impasses engendered by this solution remarkably well.

'When I say that it is in the object *a* that the sexual partner will subsequently, and always necessarily, be re-found, that is where we see a truth that is written in Genesis: the fact that the partner – and God knows, it doesn't commit her to anything – featured in the myth as being Adam's rib, so therefore the object *a*. This is why things have gone so badly ever since, with regard to this imagined perfection of the conjunction of two jouissances. In truth, I am quite sure, it is from this initial simple recognition that there emerges the necessity of an intermediary constituted by the channels of fantasy . . .'
Jacques Lacan, *The Psychoanalytic Act*, seminar of 21 February 1968.

Chapter 1

The universe of sexual laws

Since time immemorial, and across the whole range of civilisations, certain sexual prescriptions have organised the modalities of the social bond between the sexes, and have constituted what we may call sexual laws. Not so long ago, it became apparent in our own society that such a bond is distinct from an actual relation between two sexes, because it articulates only one sex as subject with the other as object. The sexual law, which was intended to establish a relation between the sexes that could not be inscribed in a discourse, does not determine what Lacan described as a 'sexual relation', in the sense of something that would articulate the desires and the jouissances of the two sexes together.

From the moment when this law lost its universal import in the Western world, it became the responsibility of psychoanalysis to show which problem that law had been responding to, what it was aiming to deal with, what could be substituted for it, and the conditions necessary for an actual sexual relation. However, this does not mean that we are studying a structure, independent of the unconscious, which would be solely responsible for a repression and an alienation bearing down on the subjects it imposes itself upon, because the law itself emerged from a formation of the unconscious, as we shall see at each stage of our exploration. But the unconscious can be interpreted and reshaped when the interpretation hits home.

The question of the 'sexual relation' is central to psychoanalysis, because it concerns everything that the unconscious has to say about sex, even though the unconscious does not actually elaborate this relation as such, and instead substitutes a collection of significations for it that do not really constitute a relation between the two sexes. The 'sexual relation' is just as present at the centre of what is dealt with in psychoanalysis as it is absent from what the unconscious elaborates. The unconscious had to wait a long time for psychoanalysis to take on the task; and that is not without its reasons.

Freud, by studying the manifestations and the laws of the unconscious according to the diachronic nature of a subject from the point of its emergence, opened up the field of a new discipline. At the centre of the elaborations of psychical functioning, he placed a construction of the personality based on unconscious elements that are encountered, confronted, processed and repressed in childhood, in order to integrate oneself as a subject in civilised society. He showed that the personality

DOI: 10.4324/9781003285984-2

is constructed in a logical fashion on the basis of successive propositions that are encountered in the infant's experience, some of which are actively forgotten and others retained. These comprise the manifestations of an infantile sexuality both autoerotic and phantasmatic, which up to this point had not been recognised in a scientific way, even if it was well-known to educators and religious instructors.

The elaboration of sexuality in psychoanalysis was thus based on its construction in the infant psyche. Incestuous desires were revealed in the unconscious, along with their conflicted relation to prohibition or to the impossible, based on sexual drives awakened before the infant's entry into language, in the relation with the original caregiver. And then these desires had to be given up, when the realisation dawned that they were forbidden by the Law, generally represented by the father; and so the accession to subjectivity was achieved. Nothing tragic, then, in the emergence and the destiny of the incestuous drives; all very logical, and no need to murder the father, except in a phantasy intended to assure oneself that there actually is a father who forbids.

Freud gave this the name of Sophocles' Oedipus, where the murder of the father was part of the tragic action; and this introduced an aspect of the process that was not inherent in it, but was all the more present the less its function was guaranteed. On the other hand, it might well appear to be a myth that a young child, broadly dependent on the desire of a mother who has complete control of its life, would be able to demonstrate the subjective freedom necessary to desire her, beyond what would consist in responding to her desire. Indeed, such a subject is mythical, but that in no way prevents it from being fundamental, since it is based on this forbidden desire just as the Cartesian cogito is based on thinking.

This is why a re-working of this structure by Lacan, in the middle of the last century, restored its real logic, showing that the child becomes established psychically at the very earliest stage, in the alienation from those on whom it depends, according to the desire of the mother. Then a prohibiting function intervenes in the name of the Father, whatever form that might take, in the place of the mother, to prevent the child from becoming completely subjected to her, and enabling a symbolic separation from her. The fact that the child complies totally with the mother's desire is already incestuous and therefore forbidden, and this is before there is even any involvement of the child's own drives. The Oedipus complex in the form of the repressed incestuous desire of a subject results from prohibition rather than struggling against it, a sort of last stand for the subject of the unconscious before repression takes place.

The psychoanalytic formulation of sexuality, then, was based on infantile sexuality as prohibited, and the first concepts were formed according to the two logical facets of the construction of the subject – alienation and separation – that are not limited to the Freudian Oedipus complex. In this sense, the child is father to the man, and in the adult unconscious what we are dealing with are the consequences of the primordial logical operations that led to the birth of subjectivity.

But restricting ourselves to this formulation represents a paradox, which consists in defining the symbolisation of human sexuality only on the basis of the time and place in childhood during which it is forbidden, or even impossible. This comes down to constructing the conceptual basis of the sexual relation only on cases from which it is fundamentally absent. In this sense, this conceptualisation gathered together what was taken for granted during a time when the Christian prohibition extended well beyond childhood and the law of incest, and authorised sex only within a strict institutional framework. Freud, indeed, considered that Christianity had done a great deal for love simply by forbidding it, because in doing so its value was increased.

So the neurotics who took part in the elaboration of this sexuality around the turn of the 20th century had no difficulty in perceiving themselves as existing in the field of a repressed sexuality, even though the genesis of their neurosis was not entirely attributable to the repression. And Freud was able to describe a whole inventory of the preoccupations of Western sexuality of that century, noting that the prohibition imposed by civilised sexual morality that weighed down on sexuality was condemning it to tip over into neurosis on a fairly frequent basis. He emphasised that the restriction it was subject to, being reserved only for the married state, led men into autoerotic and perverse practices, and women into the most colossal inhibition, which was responsible for the general weakening of feminine performance throughout the whole range of civilisations. To this he added that when, eventually, it was allowed, this sexuality was no longer particularly powerful, since inhibition had taken over on one side, and perversion on the other, and besides there was the fear of procreation in a context where contraception barely existed. From then on, if desire was to be aroused, for the woman there remained nothing but a relation of a forbidden nature, and for the man nothing but a perverse relation involving the debasement of the object. This is how he described the state of sexuality in our civilisation, as it grappled with a prohibition that was still widespread, within a powerful symbolic system, along with everything that derived from this, such as arousing desire, the 'will to understand', etc.

Even if Freud did not explicitly say so, these elements implied that fundamentally, Western Christian society, along with all its institutions, maintained an Oedipal logic, in so far as it fell entirely under a symbolic system based on the function of the Father at all levels of its structures. While the intention was to forbid all sexuality outside marriage and the family, it ended up endowing conjugal union with an imaginary allure of a legal incest, the locus of its original prohibition.

In psychoanalysis, no other symbolisation of the sexual relation has been described so far apart from that which occurs through prohibition, with its concomitant transgression and punishment, whereas one might have expected it to be represented and inscribed as a relation between the symbols of each sex. For speaking beings, prohibition symbolises the sexual, in a very obvious way in Christianity, where it was accentuated to a far greater degree, but also much earlier in the pagan world of ancient Greece, with the myths involving incest and its punishment.

In psychoanalysis, a practice which proceeds specifically by re-reading the successive constructions of subjective logic, it is perfectly valid to conceive of the psychical organisation of sexuality from the departure point of childhood, when it is forbidden; but this has a range of massive consequences that derive from the very manner in which the process is carried out. The concepts are constructed on the basis of the way they intervene in childhood, so that they are applied to a sexuality which retains some of them in a state of repression, without allowing any reference for a possible sexuality. Prohibition conditions what is felt as possible, and pathology throws light on what is normal rather than the other way round. This is certainly how Freud understood it when he wrote about civilisation and its discontents in these terms, making a leap in thinking that was to break with the ideas of degeneracy that were current at the time.

These days, when we look afresh at these facts, in a context of clinical experience marked by the developments that have taken place in our Western societies in the register of sexuality since the middle of the last century, we can begin to take the measure of the upheavals that have occurred since Freud's observations at the beginning of psychoanalysis. At this time when sexuality has been 'liberated', and is no longer based on prohibition, or restricted to the institution of marriage, when inhibition is no longer insisted upon in feminine sexuality, and the man no longer has to wait, Freud's grim view of civilised sexual morality seems to have been shattered. The sexual law no longer has the force of law, even though it remains the major reference. Once the prohibition has been reduced logically to apply to incest alone, once its extension beyond this frontier has flowed like floodwater back into a riverbed, a host of difficulties have disappeared; not, however, those that relate to sexuality as such.

The supplementary schemas elaborated by Lacan have been added on to the system of the Oedipus complex, centred on its function of the Father, which nonetheless remains pivotal. When a system that has long been presented as universal proves in fact to be relative and partial, it may seem that it should disappear completely and make way for all the other possibilities. In reality, it has not disappeared, but several modalities, other names of the Father, are now in place to ensure the distribution of the symbols and jouissances of the two sexes. In the psychoanalysis promulgated by Freud and his followers, there was a single determining facet constituted by the Oedipus complex; to this has been added another determining facet, which while being articulated with the Oedipus complex, is independent of it. In reality, the purely Oedipal determination of subjectivity and sexuality represents only what had been established as the universal masculine modality of sexuation, whereas the other facet represents the particular feminine modality. Regardless of anatomical sex, each subject can now choose to position themselves in the one or the other field.

Where the other, non-Oedipal logic of sexuation is concerned, the logical construction of a subject is not understood as an effect of childhood, in a subjective diachronicity, but rather according to the synchronous confrontation with the other sex, according to the 'sexual relation'. The approach to the other sex is no longer limited to the sexual law that emanated from the paternal system; henceforth each individual is confronted with a real relation, and has to deal with the problem that the law covered over, and can propose substitutes for and supplements to it. It is no longer a question only of concepts constructed within the universal setting of mankind's childhood, but also of those which the real of sex and the sexual relation introduce for each subject.

One of the major effects of the developments in our society has been to make the 'sexual' relation a matter of personal choice, rather than one dictated by the law, whether it is accepted or not. Although the reference to the sexual law promulgated in the Name of the Father remains present, it is no longer anything other than a single factor among others taken into consideration when determining the choice of sexuated position and sexual object. The positions exclusively prescribed by this law in the relation of one sex to the other have now revealed themselves to be impasses. They have become relativised, and no longer have the force of law, so that where they are still found to be operative, this is the result of an individual subjective choice. The element of individual choice of sexuated position and of object of desire that is now allowed means that those who make the choice have a hitherto unheard-of degree of responsibility in the face of these impasses, but also in the pathways they choose to find a way through them. While these developments have not altered the principles of psychoanalysis, they have broadly changed the context of the psychoanalytic clinic as well as our experience within it.

While we give the name of sexual law to the collection of rules organising the symbolic roles of each sex, and their relation within a given society, such a law clearly results from a symbolic construction, even if it is so ancient and ingrained that it has been taken for a natural law. Indeed, since time immemorial civilisations have defined the sexual roles symbolically, and the symbols are so powerful that we often forget that they are symbols, and believe that they represent the natural order of things. They have been constructed in the so-called collective unconscious in order to form religious and political systems, and until very recently the logic of this sexual law occupied all discourses active in the unconscious of every individual throughout their entire childhood, even if some room was left for whatever could emerge in the spaces between the loops of that net.

One of Freud's discoveries was to have begun to identity and explore this logic, and as a result over the course of the century it became apparent that it had only the remotest relation to nature. Since then this observation has passed into the public discourse, and nowadays it is widely acknowledged that there is a distance between a sexual role that would be natural and the role that is defined symbolically by the law. Each subject either fits in or does not – regardless of which sex they belong to – as has been observed in psychoanalysis and taken up in any number of schools of thought.

I. From the law prohibiting incest to the sexual law

The law regulating the relation between the sexes has been presented as a natural law, and it has not therefore been deemed to have any source other than the facts that organise their relation in nature. However, at the beginning of the last century, psychoanalysis discovered that the fundamental law of the human race, the prohibition of incest, had determining effects on sexuality, and began to show that the relation between the sexes is conditioned just as much by this prohibition. Before psychoanalysis, it had never been supposed that the law prohibiting incest would have had any incidence on the symbolic organisation of the relation between man and woman in civilised societies; and yet they are very closely linked. The law organising the relation between the sexes decrees that it must be as far away as possible from the relation between a man and his mother, and this means that the object of desire for a man is a whore rather than a mother. The greater the difference between the object of desire and the primary incestuous object, the less concern there is for the prohibition, and vice versa. Christianity took the supposed proximity of woman to the incestuous object very far indeed, so that the waves of prohibition extended well beyond their legitimate scope.

So we can say that in the beginning was the Law: that of the prohibition of incest. This law was hardly written down at all, but nonetheless universal, and psychoanalysis drew out all its consequences by revealing that the incestuous desire of infancy is given up, but also reinforced, by this very prohibition, and this is integral to the construction of subjectivity. The baby's first sensual impulses are logically directed towards the person who feeds and takes care of them, and once the prohibition is encountered, in whatever manner, those impulses are structured in the form of desire, which is repressed. The subject of the unconscious is none other than the one born of the assumption of the prohibition of incest, in the encounter with sex and language. From then on, the object that has been forbidden and renounced constitutes a lost object, and it is on the basis of this primary loss of jouissance that future desires and objects are constructed, which will compensate for the loss without themselves being subject to the prohibition. The symbolic roles of man and woman and their relation within the domain of the sexual law, seem to be broadly shaped by the law of incest rather than by any natural complementarity that could be compared to anatomical or physiological complementarity. The incidence of language on human behaviour is such that it can subvert even those natural complementarities, reorganising them into entirely different processes.

The law of the prohibition of incest arouses Oedipal desire through the encounter with its symbolic penalty. And the symbolic system of the law of the Father puts into place a very precise logic, to ensure that the prohibition will be respected, using a fundamental concept. Freud described the decisive role of the phallic symbol in the unconscious, exhuming it from the tradition of ancient Greece, where it was a perfectly conscious and present symbol in the public sphere, signifying the power, desire and fertility of a god or a human being. In our own time, this signification has become entirely implicit and silent, since the signifier has been excluded from all discourses and subjected to repression through the establishment of Christian civilisation. It has retained this signification in the unconscious, where it is omnipresent in the subject's phantasies, dreams and desires, and just as much so in the collective representations that regulate the sexual roles: everyone knows that being a man is judged in terms of having the phallus as symbol, and that being a woman is judged in terms of being the phallus as object of desire.

The symbolic order founded on the signifier of the Father, elevated as the sole possessor of this symbol, establishes a strategy to guarantee that the prohibition of incest is respected. It requires that the emerging subject who represents the symbol of what is desirable for the mother should have no right whatsoever to have it or use it for her. As a result, the subject eventually has to make a choice, according to an exclusive alternative, between the position that consists in having the phallus, and in that case not being it, or in not having it, in order to be it. Where the symbolic object of desire is concerned, a choice has to be made between being it and having it. There is a logic functioning here which means that one who occupies the position of the desirable, the object of desire of the other, cannot at the same time occupy the position of the one who desires, of the subject of desire.

It is an efficacious and simple logic, but its effect it to skew the relation in one direction. If it operates in isolation, it implies a perpetual failed encounter, because if the object of desire does not also desire the one who desires them, then no actual relation is possible. This division into the one who desires and the one who is desired is what the sexual law prescribes between man and woman, and it allows for only one who can desire. So on this basis, each subject is determined according to whether they adopt or repudiate the law of their sex, partially or totally.

This logic of an exclusive alternative engendered by the system of the Name of the Father is the same as the one that organises the symbolic positions of each sex in the unconscious and in civilisation. The girl has no object of desire in order to become it, and the boy is not it in order to be able to have it later on. She who is it may not have it, and he who has it may not be it; this enables the logical exclusion of the case where the one who has it could also be it for the mother. For one of the sexes, becoming a subject consists in ceasing to be this symbol for the mother, and then in preparing oneself to have it; for the other, it means returning, in part, to being it.

In this system, the lack of the phallus aims to prepare the girl for becoming it in the future exchange of the sexes, and the boy for having it when the time comes. In both cases, the masculine and feminine positions can only become fixed once the point has been reached where the infant has given up being the phallus, renouncing the satisfaction of the mother's jouissance, in other words, at the point where the prohibition of incest, understood in this way, has been integrated and taken on. The girl's position in the sexual law involves her ultimately returning to the position of the desirable one, in order to make herself the object of desire for the man rather than the mother. However, in our time she knows that this is only one part of her jouissance, that she will only return to it by choice, and that it will not sum her up entirely. Thus the sexual law, which has nowadays been relativised, seems to have emerged from the way in which the logical system of the Father ensured that the prohibition of incest was respected, but extended it far beyond the bounds of real incest.

II. All-phallic logic of the system of the Name of the Father

The dialectic of exchanges, of everything that consists in giving or taking within the relation to someone else – and the complex circulation between the two – all of this is organised around an implicit signification which is never spoken as such, but operates in the unconscious just as if it had been. By giving something, one places oneself implicitly in a position of the one who has something in relation to another who lacks it, and when one receives something, one positions oneself according to the lack of what one receives. Or, in a more complex way, one may give something in order to prove that one has it, or refuse to receive something because that would constitute the admission of a lack. Or again, in a different way, one may give something one does not have. This entire symbolic dialectic of exchanges has what is called the phallus as its unconscious signification, whether as a symbol or as a signifier. Indeed, it would suffice to add 'the phallus' as object/complement to all the following verbs: to give, to receive, to have, to lack, and even to be, or to fail to be, in order to capture the symbolic signification of what is at stake here.

Psychoanalysis, having been aware of the presence of this symbol in the formations of the unconscious for a long time, went on to study its signification and its logic, which are precipitated and inscribe themselves over the course of an analysis. Psychoanalytic literature described the sensual impulses of the young child towards the mother, and then towards the father who separates them; it showed that once incestuous desire had been given up or repressed, the desire of the child, and later of the adolescent, was orientated on the basis of positions dictated by the sexual law, whether or not the individual refused or adopted them. These positions are nothing other than a simple and exclusive organisation between having and being the object of desire, whether it is equivalent to being the phallus or failing to be it. In this situation, how can the symbol of the one who desires also be the symbol of the one who is desirable? In circumstances where what represents something for someone comes also to represent that someone, a specific signifying process is taking place, which Lacan termed a perverse organisation of our symbolic system, in so far as the perverse structure is formed in the same way, through inversion. This signifying organisation is not the work of particular subjects but it is in our signifying system in its entirety, and this has a number of consequences.

A great deal of doubt has been cast on the possible existence of incestuous desire of the child for the mother, or even for the father, because there is no spoken evidence of it; and the incestuous dreams of analysands cannot be taken as proof. In order to understand it, we have to emphasise that such a desire, other than in pathological cases, is formed only retroactively, as it were unconsciously.

It is only once the child has been separated from maternal desire by the paternal prohibition that they can become animated by this desire. This serves them in a way as a defence against subjective alienation, and allows separation to take place because they can use this forbidden desire as a support. In this sense, we are really talking about a mythical subject, aiming at an unreal object animated by a desire in the future perfect tense. It is not enunciated as 'I desire that', but, 'I will have desired that, which has gone'. This is the form in which is it often rediscovered in psychoanalysis with adults.

The sexual drives in the baby's first relation to the caregiver were a simple result of the sensuality of their desire, and will later be retroactively transformed into a forbidden desire tied to a lost object. This desire may also be transferred on to the father, or may be displaced on to a brother or sister, and in such cases they will also be forbidden and lost objects. Primary jouissance is necessarily lost, and this loss constitutes the basis on which future objects will be elaborated; they compensate for the lost jouissance and in some way take its place, even though in some cases they have absolutely nothing in common with it.

So even if the object takes on the appearance of a natural object of desire when it involves the desire of a man for a woman, it is not formed naturally but symbolically. We get a sense of this when we realise that normal desire comprises perverse elements – for example fetishistic ones – and this demonstrates explicitly that it aims at a symbol. It is inscribed in a structure which has several stages, where the mother as object is to the father that which the child is for the mother; this is the very principle of a hierarchical organisation of meaning. In the sexual law, the woman is the object for the man which through an inversion has been substituted for the primary incestuous object.

All of this symbolisation is based on the signification of the phallus in the unconscious. Psychoanalysis observed that the phallic symbol signified what is desirable, because primarily it symbolises the desire of the mother. In the system founded on the Name of the Father, on the basis of a declared equivalence between the phallus and the penis, the girl is identified as a being who lacks it, a being who is 'naturally' castrated, in order to receive it symbolically from a being who 'naturally' has it, initially the father, and then the man she loves.

Through spelling out this function in the unconscious of neurotics, it was possible to discern a simple and effective dialectic: having or not having this symbol of desire, receiving it or not, risking losing it, etc., which, according to the logic of this system, constituted the foundation of sexual difference between masculine and feminine, and thus the relation between them. The symbol of the phallus, constructed in ancient Greek and later Roman civilisation, and then massively repressed in Christian civilisation through becoming a signifier, organises a definition of the two sexes by means of a plus and a minus. We are thoroughly familiar with this kind of dialectic, and it seems to have been there for ever. But it can only take on a 'natural' appearance in so far as the symbol of the object of desire has become conflated with the organ whose erection is the sign of desire. The phallus is not the penis, but it is the signifier of desire, and includes the desirable one as well as the one desiring; and thus it constitutes the feminine sex as well as the masculine.

In the logical system based on the Name of the Father, the equivalence established between the penis as organ, belonging to only one of the two sexes, and the phallus as symbol or as signifier of desire has led to a confusion – even quite often in psychoanalysis – between the woman's desire for the phallus and penis envy, and between the desire to receive the organ and the desire for the possession of the organ, whereas this confusion in fact only occurs in certain cases of neurosis. Lacan reckoned that considering a woman to be castrated of an organ she had never possessed in the first place was nothing other than a denegation. Conflating the penis and the phallus, and desire and envy, has many consequences. The one who represents the name of the Father is the only one in this system to possess the phallus, and yet it can move between the sexes. This signifying system makes the phallus, as symbol of the desire of the mother, come to represent both what the child is for her and what the child comes to desire. The signification constructed on this basis covers all subjects and all objects of desire, in a binary mode, as when one would use 0 to denote the one who is castrated, and 1 for the one who is not, in the registers of having and being. This is the logical principle at the heart of the construction of discourse and its inscription.

The sexual law renews the logic of the exclusive alternative between being and having by redistributing between man and woman the being and having that was shared out in childhood between mother, child, and father. This can be translated into what consists for one sex in being the object of desire without having it, or, for the other, of having the object of desire without being it. This is how, in the course of the 20th century, the logics that had produced the formations of the unconscious relating to sex were brought to light, as our civilisations had enforced them. When Freud established that the child symbolised the entire group of sexuated living beings with the help of the symbol of a single organ, some having it and others not, he qualified it with the infantile logic of the phallic phase, which operates on the simple basis of its presence or its absence, considered as a lack.

The sexual law at work in civilisations appeared to function according to a comparable principle. Exclusively based throughout millennia on the statement 'you are the one who has, you have the one who is', it implied that the one and the other were complementary as a subject is complemented by its object. The powerful incidence of the Name of the Father of religion in society, as the agent of the prohibition of incest, and then of all sexual jouissance, linked the logic of the sexual law to a position of Oedipal filiation, where all are deprived of jouissance apart from the one who enforces the prohibition.

This function of the phallus serves to disengage the child from maternal alienation, opposing to it the law of the one who alone is supposed/assumed to have it. But it is formed according to a logic of the 'all' that is not necessary to produce this effect. Ancient Greece represented a tragic trajectory from being the phallus as the incestuous son, the jouissance of the Mother Goddess, to having the phallus, exclusively, as the Father of Olympus, in a variety of ways. Where the relation between the sexes was concerned, a symbolic organisation of this kind, which Christianity integrated by repressing it, had radical consequences for the functioning of the institutions of civilisations that lasted thousands of years. The very fact that Freud described this system during the last century has contributed to its being challenged in those very societies where it held sway; and in our time it has already been severely shaken up.

The sexual law cannot be defined solely in terms of infantile narcissism or the Oedipal dialectic, because it also bears on the real of the adult sexual relation. The current rebuttal of this law and its consequences has contributed to the establishment of a new situation. There is no longer a universal definition of lack or possession according to one's anatomical sex, but rather each individual self-determines according to a subjective choice, adopting or refusing, partially or entirely, the positions defined for each sex. The phallus has been detached from the equivalence with the penis as organ.

This has happened to the extent that the penis is no longer the referent for the phallus, and each subject makes an unconscious choice as to having it or not, being it or not, and acts accordingly in professional and social registers as well as in the sexual sphere. Popular discourse expresses this in terms of who 'wears the trousers' in a couple. The phallus has appeared as a symbol that can pertain to either sex, in one way or another on a case-by-case basis, so that each individual, whichever their sex, can self-define according to their own choice. What is more, it has been shown that the phallic symbol no more determines the whole of a human being than it determines all human beings according to the universality of their sex. It may be lacking at one point in subjective structure, for example, in the social or professional register, while being present in the sexual register, or the converse may be true; the two points finding a way of knotting so as to link with each other.

Nonetheless, the phallus remains the basic symbol of desire in the unconscious, of the one who desires and of the one who is desirable, and desire organised according to the positions of the traditional sexual law continues to play a major part. Although it involves a considerable number of impasses, which have been identified, this law constitutes a real logic, and conditions a powerful form of desire. Even though a range of other modalities of desire have appeared, there can be no doubt that masculine desire continues to be caused and supported to a large extent by the feminine as object, whether it is equivalent to the phallus or not, and feminine desire continues to be constructed with the aim of being desired or not. And there are still frequent cases of what Freud identified at the beginning of the last century, where the man's desire is only aroused by a 'debased' feminine object, while his love goes to a woman who reminds him of his mother, idealised but not desired; and where feminine desire can only really flourish in circumstances of prohibition.

The fact that this law is no longer the only player in the game of the organisation of desires is no reason to dismiss its terms completely. When something that had been posited as universal becomes relativised, its universal character may disappear, but not the fact of its existence. The way this law has been revised has had considerable effects; it has eliminated some sexual difficulties, and created new ones. Because its universality has been threatened and it no longer represents the only relation possible between the sexes, the law has become radicalised in certain extreme cases, whether in individual subjects or in politico-religious groups.

III. 'Complementary' relations between the sexes

It is still essential to grasp the principle of functioning of the sexual law, since the fact that it no longer has universal scope does not mean that it no longer constitutes a fundamental point of reference. Although it no longer determines everything in the symbolic order where sex is concerned, this does not mean that it no longer determines anything at all. One cannot think of what is in question here in terms of 'all or nothing'. Maintaining an order where not everything is orientated according to the same logic is characteristic of the way things are evolving in our time, and consequently many facts that were formerly presented in terms of 'either this or that' are now presented in non-exclusive terms: 'sometimes this, sometimes that'. Maintaining a position in this is difficult, since mainstream discourse generally aspires to universals.

From time immemorial, the law has prescribed the terms according to which each individual should approach the fields of love and the sexual relation, and even at the beginning of the last century they were still regulated and organised by the structures of kinship and marriage that overlaid them. The signifying and economic system prevailing at the time did not allow for couples to be formed on the basis of love, except in exceptional circumstances, and would not tolerate the undoing of a marriage between lineages. Besides, there is a certain nostalgia for the time when someone decided on behalf of each individual which man or woman they should spend their life with, without any expectation of love, which proved fragile and unreliable as a basis for marriages and families. Even though this nostalgia does not in any way represent a real desire to go back in time, and knowing in any case that this would not be possible, it does on the other hand show the considerable weight of responsibility now borne by each individual in determining the direction and modalities of their life. It increases the impact of neurosis and of the failures in life's choices. Indeed, psychoanalysis by definition only encounters those for whom something has gone wrong, while those who do not enter into psychoanalysis often organise themselves in a satisfactory way according to one system or another; but the symptoms of the former bear witness to something that is true for all.

In the choices made in the sphere of love, and without any guide other than the conscious and unconscious desire of each individual and that desire's compatibility with that of the other, we can now assess what remains of the phallic dialectic that is fundamental to the constitution of the relation between the sexes. We can establish that a number of women still broadly approach the relation to the other sex via the desire of the man, by offering themselves as object, while a number of men still approach the woman as object of desire. This observation shows the extent to which the traditional sexual law remains an essential reference, but is has nonetheless become relativised, since we can now establish that the original distribution of both desire and the object are no longer universal.

Some men cannot orientate themselves sexually unless they are desired, and certain women can only do so by choosing the object they desire; and this no longer places them outside the law. In very many cases, the sexuated position and the choice of object develop over the course of a lifetime by passing from one side to the other. This means that what could be called the man's fetishistic relation to desire, which conditions the way he approaches the other sex as object, and the erotomanic relation of the woman to desire, which conditions her approach to the other sex as desire, have broadly persisted without, however, being universal, and without involving the totality of the being of desire. This question of desire and the object appears in the same way in homosexual relations.

In Western societies, this sexual law is no longer a law as such, even if, tragically, it has been radicalised in certain parts of the world. The consequences of its phallic dialectic have largely been relativised in so far as they are no longer universally imposed. A woman may now find her worth in many ways, whereas for so long the principal way of doing so was through becoming the object of desire and love, with all the anxiety this entailed in having to position herself as object of desire when faced with the desire of the Other. For the man, approaching a woman as object initially involved presenting himself as desiring, and therefore lacking, and then required that he should give her what she herself lacked; but now this gift is nothing other than a subjective choice, and in no way imposed on him, even if paradoxically it is demanded when separations occur. The impasses that emerge in these relations that are 'complementary' in terms of subject and object are still present even when the relation is established in this way, but they are now experienced as arising from particularities rather than universalities in discourse. This does not mean that they are any easier to overcome. It is no longer considered to be the law for one sex to present itself as object of desire, lacking the phallus in order to be it, or indeed the law of the other sex not to be the phallus in order to have it; the choice of sexuated position and of object pertain uniquely to each individual, to each pair. It is unconscious subjective construction that determines the choice, depending on who is encountered; anatomical sex is one attribute among many, and a sexual law is relative, no longer constituting a destiny.

The discourse of sexual law propounded a complementarity of the sexes, but not just any one. Certainly there is a natural, biological and anatomical complementarity, and one might expect the law to be content with interpreting that particular form. In fact it does something quite different: it interprets the symbolic complementarity constructed on the relation of a subject to their object through the phallic dialectic of the relation. The complementarity reflected in the law according to the phallic function has nothing to do with reproduction – at least not explicitly – but rather with the metaphor of Genesis, as in 'one flesh'. Genesis contributed to the establishment of this symbolic relation of the phallic function by initially making Eve a lost part of the man's body: she was extracted from him in the form of a rib, and given back to him in the form of a woman. This extraction/subtraction made the primordial man incomplete, so refinding an equivalent was supposed to make him complete once again. This is the type of complementarity at stake in the formulation, 'the man is the one who has, and what he has is what is: the feminine object'. So a type of complementarity can be based, however falsely, on the extraction of a part, and then the refinding of an object that takes its place, thus giving the idea of a whole. This myth is an essential factor in the all-phallic logic to which the law contributes.

This complementarity is based on one single desire, in its relation to the object of the desire. The position of one sex is defined as the desire to desire, and of the other as the desire to be desired; it means that desire is unilaterally on one side, and the object on the other. The 'complementarity' of the sexual law consists in splitting the functions of desire in two, and placing them separately on either side of the sexes – the object of desire on one side, and its subject on the other. There is nothing sexual about it, since being or having a symbol does not involve anything inherently sexual, but merely determines the signification of one body in relation to another when they come together in the name of the law.

Freud noted that masculine sexuality was reinforced by the repression of feminine sexuality, and he had initially deduced from this that there was one single libido that was represented – the masculine libido defined by the phallus. He later established that if there is indeed only one, it is no more masculine than it is feminine, and one could even say it is asexual. It is now broadly accepted that this libido defined by the symbol of the phallus is indeed no more masculine than feminine, since women participate in phallic jouissance just as much as men, not only where speaking and maintaining a position in speech is concerned, but also at the purely physical level in terms of clitoral jouissance. The way the unconscious processes it is the same, that is, having jouissance of the phallus whether you possess it or not.

In those societies where the sexual law had currency, its symbolic organisation was accompanied logically by an insistence on the virginity of the woman. Since the object of desire represented the symbol of marriage, of the exchange of one lineage with another, to retain its value meant not sustaining any sort of loss in a relation other than that of the marriage, and the transmission of phallic value to the other lineage took place, ultimately, through the sexual relation.

However, even at the time when the so-called complementary relation between man and woman was far more influential as a sexual law, Freud had noticed contradictory elements in the way it functioned, which led him already to think that it was not the whole story about the relation between man and woman. Initially he had found that the most widespread choice of object for women was to be loved more than to love, whereas for men it was to love more than to be loved; and this seemed to confirm or indeed apply the schema of the law. But this fact was later complicated by the observation that the man's choice was more often the woman who feeds than the narcissistic woman, and this contradicted the two modalities that had been observed earlier on. And so suddenly a difficulty was revealed in the study of the sexual relation in psychoanalysis: a non-conjunction at one point, which required some clever footwork.

Whereas at the time of these observations, it seemed that approaching the other sex via the sexual law might suffice to form the basis of a sexual relation – in other words an actual and sexual relation between two partners of two sexes – it has clearly been shown since then that this is not the case, across the entire social spectrum. The very idea of complementarity has been profoundly shaken by the collapse of the universality of the sexual law. Since it now appears to have been a fiction based on a hierarchical organisation between the sexes that has been challenged in our time, the question is what can come into its place to form the basis of a relation between them. The so-called complementary relation nonetheless remains a reference, and the construction of a real relation between the two sexes does not consist in rejecting it, but rather in adding something to it, as we shall see.

IV. This is not a 'sexual relation'

Complementarity is what makes a relation, yet the relation that is based on sexual law cannot be called sexual in the sense of involving two sexes, because it concerns only one of them and its object. However, it can be called sexuated. The way Lacan used the term 'sexual relation', with its double meaning, emphasises the play on words, leading us to wonder whether the sexual act does in fact determine a relation between them. Exploring the full meaning of each word, he further questioned whether or not there was a relation there, in the sense of something that can be written, of a proportion between two terms, and whether or not this relation was actually sexual, in the sense of something that involves two sexes. If we allow the whole weight of this questioning to bear on each of the terms of this expression, along with all the concepts that it is based on, we see a considerable range of variables issuing from it. Such a relation may well be a relation, but cannot be sexual in the sense that it does not involve two sexes, or does not involve sexuality. Such a relation which is actually sexual between two partners of the two sexes cannot be written as a relation, in the sense that it is not part of discourse.

The richness of the word play around this expression shows that it is precisely the fact that if we take each of the terms in the fullest sense of what they imply, there is no such thing as a 'sexual relation' that can be written. Because there is no case in which all the occurrences of the expression can be brought together. The 'complementary' relation promulgated as a sexual law is not one of them, because although it can be deemed to be sexuated, it cannot be sexual, and the relation that is sexual in this sense cannot be written in discourse, whereas many others which are not sexual can be. From this point on, an ironic tone appears in relation to the expression: contrary to what is enunciated in language, and what might seem to proven simply by a sexual act, sex does not form a relation. We might well laugh at this, and demonstrate that there certainly is a sexual relation, in the form of coitus, but we will have proved nothing of the sort, and the provocative nature of the aphorism alerts us to what is truly implied by the expression, going to the very heart of what civilisation has failed to achieve.

The problematic effects of the 'complementary' relation determined by the phallic function have now been widely recognised far beyond the field of Freudian/ Lacanian psychoanalysis. They can be deduced from the text of the founding metaphor, that of Genesis, and the discourse that flowed from the time of its origin, distributing jouissances in a specific way. Since the moment when this metaphor began to organise the formation of the human couple, through the extraction of a part of the man to form his feminine object, the object itself has been defined as a part of him, and therefore, logically, the jouissance he obtains from it will be autoerotic. This jouissance will not then be able to provide the basis for a relation of two, a 'sexual relation'. The symbol of the phallus simply confers its signification on the feminine object, which comes to take the place of the object that has been extracted. According to the logic inaugurated on the basis of the metaphor of Genesis, in the encounter with the woman the man merely refinds his bodily complement – the woman completes him with a part of himself. This complementarity is based on the assumption of a body that has had an organ cut out of it, not on the existence of another jouissance. It actually corresponds to what we can observe concerning traditional traits of virility based on this law of discourse, since these traits are organised entirely around the possession of the phallus, the symbol of power, or of the woman.

The effects of this logic can be found in what Freud described as the woman's narcissistic preference – to be loved – and that of the man – to love. However, the complication this entailed, given that he noted that the man's choice was often of the woman 'who feeds', which was elaborated in his study of 'The universal tendency to debasement in the sphere of love', showed that there was something else determining the man's choice, governed by a polarising spilt. At one pole is the autoerotic jouissance achieved through the feminine object, and that is not where love is to be found; and at the other is idealised love, and that is not where desire is to be found. This splitting between a sensual current and an affectionate current, which has been observed since the beginnings of psychoanalysis, is partly conditioned by the avoidance of the prohibition of incest, since within that framework, to love a woman one also desires, or to desire a woman one also loves, would consist in reuniting the two currents; and that would be felt to be incestuous in so far as they were separated by the primary prohibition of incest. The prohibition of being the phallus if one has it, and of having it if one is it, which is how the system of the Name of the Father translates this fundamental law into logic, extends this prohibition of incest far beyond its real borders, multiplying the impasses, which cannot be avoided directly, but only with the help of detours.

This 'complementary' relation that links the man to the feminine object corresponds logically to a myth, constructed by the child at the time of the birth of subjectivity, of an all-powerful Father. This symbolic Father is the one who is capable of restraining the desire of the mother, who herself is all-powerful where the child is concerned. He can have jouissance of her at will, without castration and without limits, and thus, through the inauguration of an Other of the Other, enables the child to cease being completely subjected to maternal desire. These days, the law no longer supports such a construction of the powers of the head of the family, and as a result throughout the world we can observe an appeal to the myth of such a Father, becoming more and more violent where it appears in radical forms within extremist organisations.

Freud constructed his myth of the Father of the Horde on a logic similar to the one that aims to rein in maternal desire, since it is defined precisely by his power to have jouissance at will not of a single woman, but of all the women in the tribe, and thus of all the mothers in the eyes of their children. This is the source of the solution known as polygamy. To possess the phallus was equivalent to the possible possession of all women. And at the time when adolescents identify with a model of their sex, it is a Father of this type who is largely present in phantasy, driving them to act or, conversely, inhibiting their actions.

The sexual law of 'being the one who has and having the one who is' enunciates what the jouissance of Man might be in the name of this Father. It defines his sexual role as consisting in being the master in relation to the other sex. The way our societies are evolving nowadays has undermined this notion; it is now nothing more that a position taken up by some individuals, although it persists widely in the phantasies of both sexes, and the phantasy of the master is certainly easier to embrace now that the reality of it has been significantly reduced. The choice is no longer anything other than individual, consisting, for example, for certain women in sacrificing their own jouissance in order to participate solely in that of the man in the name of the Father.

Within this framework, when a woman sacrifices her own jouissance, her desire will be only the desire to be desired, and a prohibition of jouissance will appear in order to be represented only as a metaphor for the man's jouissance. In this there is a sort of appeal to the mythical Father, the only mode of separation that can be found in the face of a maternal law that is impossible to curb, or sometimes a desire of the real father that is too intrusive.

Some men devote themselves to sustaining the myth of such a Father in one way or another. Since this choice serves as a radical defence against the alienation in the face of a mother's subjugating desire, we can imagine that any religious belief that radicalises this myth of the Father or of God will be a refuge, tragic as it may become, for a subject who cannot find an alternative in their own culture.

The sexuated relation articulated in complementary terms by the law does not involve a meeting of jouissances of the two sexes, nor an expression of their respective desires, but rather an orientation of the sexual couple around one single desire. One of the desires cannot be deployed, one jouissance remains adrift. One party can only obtain jouissance auto-erotically through his physical complement, and the other can only be this jouissance. It is not, therefore, a sexual relation as such, since the phallic function that determines it consists in the jouissance that one subject is said to have of the other as object, rather than in the conjunction or articulation in a discourse of two jouissances. Certainly we can suppose that the relation laid down by the law did not in any way reflect the reality of sexual practices, even if there is little we can know about it, since a number of those practices have always been determined outside the terms of the discourse of the law, but it was that discourse nonetheless that orientated the practices. The sexual law has always been presented as the 'natural' relation between one sex and the other, but, right up to the last century, it masked the fact that such a relation would be something completely different. Nowadays having been widely relativised, it masks to a lesser and lesser extent the fact that a real relation between the two sexes is inscribed neither in discourse nor in the unconscious.

When old structures fall apart, it is important to grasp how this happens, so as to see what is redistributed, and how. The fact that there is no relation articulated in discourses between the sexes does not mean that none is possible, since it not difficult to observe that certain sexual couples manage to create something durable that resembles it. In all this, there is a sticking point that results first and foremost from the construction of our symbolic order.

V. What of feminine jouissance?

The 'complementary' relation laid down by the law says nothing about feminine jouissance, but rather elides it. In the course of the centuries has been interpreted in various ways, even to the extent of being outlawed. This has had, and still has, a great number of consequences, since this jouissance remains in some way affected by a prohibition emanating from the subject, which leads us to suppose, as Freud had noted, that there is a rejection of the feminine in the unconscious itself; and this needs to be looked at anew. The law has not prevented the existence in all eras of loves that have united two desires, rather than one desire and its object; there are many great love stories in history that testify to this. Feminine jouissance did not wait until the modern era to make its mark, silently, in real love relations, independently of the discourses that elided it. It is not spoken in discourse, and it is indeed difficult to speak of it because it involves a partial objection to the logic of the phallic function. It does not stand in opposition to the phallic function, nor does it refuse to accept the terms of the law, but rather adds to it, above and beyond discourse, something that contradicts it. Thus a new logic can be defined, which does not stem from the traditional logic of non-contradiction; it does not comprise an exclusive alternative, it does not proceed from the 'all'. It does not prevent the inscription of the sexual couple in the law according to the terms of the phallic function, but it does introduce something supplementary.

It is not to the sexual law as such that feminine jouissance constitutes an objection, but rather to the fact that the law determines everything, that the phallic function occupies the entire space of jouissance and defines the woman in her entirety, that the law is unique and universal. This mode of jouissance should not be confused with that of the mother, which is phallic in structure, and in this sense just as autoerotic as that of the man, constituted in the same way through the relation to the object of phantasy as a part of the subject, since the child is part of herself. Nor is feminine jouissance hysterical in nature, which would consist in reducing the woman to a metaphor of the jouissance of the man, while objecting to being it herself.

If jouissance that is specifically feminine has often been confused with the two other forms of jouissance available to women, as much in psychoanalysis as elsewhere, it is because both of the latter provide easy ways to restore and re-establish a logic of the 'all'; yet feminine jouissance positions itself outside of this. Indeed, it does not refuse to occupy the position of object of desire of the man as defined by the law, but nor does it situate itself completely within it; it adds something else, and it is not based on the alternative 'all or nothing'. It involves making oneself into an object, but above and beyond this, it is as object that she has jouissance of the Other, and that is where desire comes into play. This is where the object becomes active, and the subject is subverted, which reverses the benchmarks of classical logic.

In his seminar on 'The Purloined Letter', Lacan made use of a fiction, namely Poe's tale, to approach his elaboration of the position of this feminine jouissance in the institutions of the law, and to create a metaphor for what it was that the system of the Name of the Father subjected it to, and what is happening nowadays as it is deconstructed.[1] The purloined letter shows, silently, that there is something beyond what the law has laid down concerning the woman's jouissance, adding something to what she experiences in being the man's woman. The objection is only to the fact that this position should be her entire jouissance, and that it defines the whole of 'The' woman, according to the universal definition in the sexual law as the complement of the man. While she does not refuse to be his complement, she demonstrates that she is not just that, and that she can obtain jouissance from something else. The jouissance that is specifically feminine is not forbidden, but it simply cannot be spoken, because it is partially in contradiction to what is spoken.

When feminine jouissance is at work, it occurs in a relation involving two jouissances and two sexes rather than one, and so it goes beyond the discourse of the law. Since it has its origins in another logic than that of discourse, it can only be active outside discourse, and manifests itself in putting words into action rather than just in words. The phallic function, which makes the woman completely the object of the man's desire, is thus partially annulled, and something supplementary introduces a different relation. It constitutes something spoken that goes beyond the terms of the law in some way, without actually going beyond it, since it takes support from the law in what is spoken.

Feminist struggles have been more concerned with a recognition of women's phallic jouissance than with this other jouissance, in so far as the former is that of the subject, and in this sense is no more masculine than feminine. Orgasm here has nothing specifically feminine about it, unless we consider the transitory disappearance of the subject as being feminine. This realisation came to fruition at the end of the last century, in the majority of domains – society, the job market, love, family, sex – and brought about massive social change. But jouissance that is specifically feminine, which did not wait for contemporary developments in the relation between the sexes in order to exist, and which is added to the subject's jouissance, still remains outside discourse. Still today it has no place other than in the interstices between statements, since the latter only accept as essential the 'all' of the phallic function, in one way or another, on one side or the other of the sexes.

In Freud's first attempts to describe the vagaries of feminine jouissance, he noted that prohibition could be one of its conditions. This was the first way in which he tried tentatively to define it. In this sense, he got it right, but only partially, because the prohibited (*interdit*) cannot be superimposed on the 'between speech' (*inter-dit*), and nor is what is outside the law the same as what is outside the law of discourse. This is the point where we observe the ambiguity of Poe's tale, and the limit we come up against when we try to use it as a metaphor for the relation between man and woman, and the way this develops. By allowing us to suppose that the letter purloined from the queen mentioned a forbidden jouissance, since it had to be hidden from the king, the tale evokes a dimension other than that of a feminine jouissance, which, even if it is not spoken, is not hidden.

Note

1 Jacques Lacan, *Écrits*, New York, Norton, 2006, pp. 6–48.

Chapter 2

The experience of the sexual relation

The law that organises and prescribes the way the sexes position themselves has always been known to have an enormous impact on sexual relations, since it aims to regulate and inscribe these within the institutions of a civilisation. We may wonder to what extent each individual's real jouissances are organised by the law, and there is no way of fully knowing this. The characteristics of the sexual encounter are influenced by it, because they are in part psychically determined. However, while they do depend to a significant degree on the subjective and discursive determination of jouissances, the sexual act and the orgasm that brings it to a conclusion also have their own physiological laws. The biology of the sexual relation between man and woman includes some traits that cannot be overlooked, and upon which the discourse of the law has certain effects. Furthermore, it has become apparent that certain biological traits themselves bear on subjectivity, and may have been interpreted to provide the very basis of sexual law. Thus the idea is introduced of a two-way interaction between language and the body, between the psychical and the organic. But first of all, let us explore the effects of the law on the sexual relation.

I. Effects of the law on the sexual encounter

It is impossible to determine precisely what the effects of the law are here, but we can discern some traces in what is said in various fields, notably in that of psychoanalytic practice, which looks at these things in a quite different way from the media. Psychoanalytic practice by definition deals with the field of the symptom and therefore only indirectly reflects individual experience; but the difficulties it is concerned with are those encountered by everyone, even if they are not treated in the same way. In our time, when the prohibitions of the law have largely loosened their grip, the first thing that strikes us is the number of cases in which those prohibitions are perpetuated, with many subjects continuing to inflict them on themselves; it is as if one has to reintroduce the prohibition oneself, when it is no longer there, as if it fulfilled a need, or brought some satisfaction.

On the other hand, the position of each individual in a sexual couple is still frequently organised according to the terms of the law that was in force,

DOI: 10.4324/9781003285984-3

unequivocally, until the middle of the last century. Feminine desire, which was elided by the law, is still frequently found not to be taken into account in the sexual encounter, just as much by the woman herself, unless it takes the form of the desire to be desired. And while their desire is far more overt nowadays, it is still the case that many women find themselves caught in the impossibility of desiring a man unless he has already shown his own desire, and can only determine their own position by giving in to that desire, or not. So what defined a woman's 'virtue' when the law was universally imposed remains an immutable logic for certain women, no longer with the force of law, but as an unconscious choice. It is not just inhibition that is involved, however, because approaching the man as desire and not as object of desire is specific to feminine desire. It is more and more frequently the case that men, too, can approach a woman only as desire, and not as object of desire. Feeling that it is impossible to initiate anything where there might previously have been an encounter unless the woman invites them to do so, and this certainly poses more problems than if it is the other way round.

From popular discourse, we are all aware that the sexual act involves an asymmetry of jouissances of the two sexes. At the organic level, the male orgasm occurs more rapidly, and it takes a long time before it can be repeated, whereas the female orgasm takes longer to occur, but then can be repeated more rapidly. Of course, there are no rules, and the sexual relation, which is a very intimate thing, cannot easily be described in general terms, but it is recognised in many discourses that there is a common tendency to dissymmetry of the bodily manifestations of masculine and feminine jouissances. So there is a difficulty on the horizon concerning the conjunction of the two; or we might even say that there is a disjunction between them, and that one jouissance often remains adrift. As a recent essay puts it, 'where the man was desperately trying *not* to reach a climax, at the same time, the woman was equally desperately trying *to* reach a climax'.[1] Is this caused solely by the effects of the sexual law, as has generally been supposed?

The way that discourses and ideas have developed has echoed the observation, made in the 1960s, that the female orgasm is often absent in intercourse, and now attention is mainly focussed on this question with the aim of dealing with it, from the perspective of both sexes, by reducing the residual effects of ideology on the sexual encounter. And there is no doubt that this has brought about major modifications in the way a sexual relation unfolds, and there is clearly less dissymmetry once there is a resolve to tackle the problem. However, even when more space has been given to feminine desire and jouissance, in its psychical and physical aspects, it remains a fact that the sexual act does not regularly bring about female orgasm. There is a fundamental dissymmetry that has been observed since time immemorial. That is no measure of feminine jouissance as such, however, because we know from the psychoanalytic clinic that an authentic jouissance does not require orgasm, although it may still be a major factor.

This remains partially linked to the effects of the sexual law. Since the law does not allude to either desire or jouissance for the woman, the woman may prohibit herself from having them in any form whatsoever. In offering oneself in the sexual encounter as the representative of the jouissance of the other, the subject assumes in the unconscious that to desire or to have jouissance is not allowed; it is not that the one whom one enjoys is not allowed to but that is how it is interpreted. We may well believe that the impact of the law, which defines masculine jouissance as having the woman at his disposal, while eliding her jouissance, plays a significant role in this well-known aspect of the sexual encounter. To this we can add the impact of religion, which initiated and extended the law, prohibiting jouissance, and authorising only the procreative relation, which in no way suffered as a result.

Within the same discourse we find the notion of making One in the sexual relation, and this is broadly underpinned by the religious metaphor 'they shall be of one flesh'. This idea of a One of union is in fact a displacement of the primary relation of the child to the mother, when the baby cannot distinguish itself from her, and feels like a part of her. In the same way, the biblical Eve was One with the man by being, according to the myth, a part of him. The One, pursued by every individual in their idea of the sexual relation, is therefore a myth, inherited from Oedipal relations in order to protect the ideal of sexual jouissance. In the real encounter, its relative failure, which is unavoidable, is experienced by each partner as a castration. It is as if becoming One in the sexual act failed because of the individual's incapacity to fulfil their role: truly having the phallus for the man, or truly being the phallus for the woman. Each feels inadequate for their role, and for each, the other is the one who castrates them. As far as 'one flesh' is concerned, instigated by Genesis along with the sexual law, where the phallic being of woman came to constitute the phallic having that man had to refind, a gap has opened up, and in the reality of the act the experience is quite different from what was expected.

In the sexual act, furthermore, the question of feminine jouissance returns, confronting each partner with the anguished and ambivalent expectation it arouses, and the search for ways in which it may be sidestepped by both. What has been elided and repressed always threaten to return, arousing anxiety in both partners. And beyond this, it evokes another jouissance that has been excluded, which is at the origin of this one: the jouissance of the mother, because the formation of the subject depended on what they had been separated from. If the sexual law is indeed inherited from what was excluded by the prohibition of incest, it must in some way be haunted in its interstices by the jouissance it forbade, as if there were always a threat that it might return; as if what had been thrown out of the door would return through the window. The Oedipal scene thus haunts the sexual act, because by its very nature it evokes each individual's first relation with the jouissance of the Other, like something repressed that the sexual law of discourse elides. Since the phallic function of the law, which organises the complementary relation of a masculine subject to a feminine object, was originally constituted by substituting this feminine object for the desiring mother, approaching the sexual act through this relation involves confronting, at least partially, what the law excluded in order to construct the relation. And since discourse does not offer a model for any kind of jouissance for the woman, once that of the mother has been excluded, she can only try to invent one *ex nihilo*.

So the sexual act seems to involve an essential difficulty: the ideal relation on the basis of which the partners approach each other differs from what they actually encounter, and this causes a certain anxiety. The entire organisation of the law, as a relation that is supposedly complementary between man and woman, involves substituting a feminine object for the all-powerful desire of the primordial Other, which everyone has had to deal with, repressing it in order to construct a self. The man's jouissance is organised around this object, whose own jouissance is elided in order for it to be distanced as far as possible from any evocation of the incestuous desire he flees from. Hence the common image of sex as involving a rather rapid and conclusive male orgasm, as opposed to the possibility for the woman of an unpredictable, slower and inconclusive orgasm. This represents an organic disjunction of their jouissances, and may initially be considered as resulting from the influence of the law on the sexual act.

We may indeed consider that there is a parallel between the expectations of the law and the way the sexual act takes place. Sexual union seems to achieve the status of a metaphor here enacting the law. From this point of view, it does not make it any easier for two jouissances to be articulated as the sexual law is based on the phallic function. At first glance, the sexual act seems to conform to what is laid down by the sexual law, where a masculine jouissance is articulated not with that of a woman but with a woman as the *object* of desire and of jouissance.

II. Non-conjunction of the jouissances of the two sexes

Unlike the early sexologists, however, Lacan was far from considering the details of the sexual act as resulting simply from the psychical effects of the sexual law. He described these details with an open mind, without prejudging what contributed to their presence. He recognised the importance of their biological dimension, which we believe to have been both justified and necessary. In the 1960s, studying various aspects of the orgasm at the juncture of the psychical and the biological, he concluded that it was there that Freud's supposed biological 'rock' underlying the castration complex was to be found. Freud, as we know, in the very last phase of his work, established the irreducibility of the woman's reaction of depression, and the man's protest, in the face of the castration complex, and suggested there was probably a biological element that was impossible to eliminate at the origin of this anxiety. As Freud wrote, 'for the psychical field, the biological field does in fact play the part of the underlying bedrock'.[2] Nowadays, this sentence still resonates powerfully.

While Lacan was turning his attention to this study of the sexual relation, American sexology, which was launched by the Kinsey report and its considerable repercussions, had contributed to the growing research indicating the frequent lack of female orgasm, its predominantly clitoral origin, and the relative rapidity of the male orgasm. A degree of disjunction was revealed between the jouissances of the man and the woman, regardless of the satisfaction experienced, which was as unanimous, by the way, as the testimony to the disjunction. Lacan certainly shared this opinion, but interpreted it in a quite different way.

First of all, he noted that one biological characteristic of the copulatory function, in humans and in some other species, was the concomitance between orgasm followed by ejaculation and detumescence, that amounted to a cut in the copulatory function in the very outcome of the orgasm. He immediately recognised the import of this, in so far as this phenomenon, which is involuntary and triggered subjectively by the unconscious, constituted the conclusive material element of intercourse for both partners. Detumescence gave a concrete form to the limit of pleasure, in the Freudian sense of the term, the threshold of the male subject's pleasure, in his relation to his own jouissance and that of the other. In this complex knot of subjectivity, desire and jouissance of the one in relation to the other, Lacan found the key to Freud's hypothesis:

> The essential relation between castration and the copulatory function has already prompted us to try – after all, following the indication of Freud, who tells us that at this level, without him justifying it in any way, however, we are touching on some biological bedrock – to articulate it as lying within a particularity of the function of the copulatory organ at the human biological level.[3]

This characteristic of human intercourse is both so central and so familiar that its consequences go unnoticed except when they get caught up in a symptom. And yet these are extensive, and in order to begin to explore them, Lacan first emphasised that the function of detumescence is in no way essential to the orgasm, and that there are numerous species in which it does not occur. The fact that it is concomitant with orgasm in our species links orgasm to a cut, a weakening, a disappearance of the copulatory organ. Once that is established, the link between the organ and anxiety in human copulation becomes obvious, as does its impact on the modalities of desire and jouissance in the sexual couple.

He further observed that this final cut intervenes at the threshold of jouissance, in the psychoanalytic sense that it is situated beyond the limit of the pleasure principle. The cut often entails a feeling of occurring too soon, which is certainly widely echoed in contemporary discourses. But in exceptional circumstances it may turn into a feeling of occurring too late, which will also define a limit to jouissance. The pathway of phallic jouissance involves a tension when confronted with the call to jouissance of the other, and there is a tendency to back off prematurely when faced with that call. There we have the basis of what Freud called the castration complex, which is in truth quite familiar in what is at stake in sexual jouissance.

This is what Lacan had to say on the subject:

> [T]he organ is never likely to hold up very far on the road along which jouissance is calling it. With regard to this aim of jouissance and to reaching this

end point, which would be tragic, evoked in the call of the Other, the amboceptive organ can be said to yield prematurely. At the moment when it could become the sacrificial object, so to speak, let's say that in the most common cases it has already yielded some time before. It's no more than a little scrap, no longer there for the partner except as a marker, a memento of tenderness. That is what the castration complex is all about.[4]

The castration complex is linked to the fact, which has always been recognised, that the male orgasm, with its ejaculation accompanied by detumescence, often happens before the woman's orgasm, and may therefore constitute an obstacle to the latter, resulting in an effect of castration for both parties. Certain sexologists consider that this trend in the biological curve is an inheritance relating to the sexuality of prehistoric man which, since he was exposed to predators, had to be quick, while the woman's sexuality was slower in nature. In reality, it is more probable that the discrepancy was destined to further the aim of fertilisation, the fertilising emission requiring a swift accomplishment, while the female orgasm is not necessary to this end. There is an obvious contradiction between the biological characteristics of the sexual act that satisfy the aim of fertilisation, which only requires one orgasm, and those of the jouissance of the sexual couple, which requires both. And it is worth emphasising that ancient civilisations took this into consideration, because some of them constructed rites designed to work against this contradiction, exploring the means to satisfy the jouissance of the couple, as in the East. Others rejected this aim of jouissance, and only retained the goal of fertilisation, which resolved the contradiction by eliding it, as was the case in Western Christianity.

Elsewhere, Lacan noted that it is very rare to find objective signs of female orgasm throughout the animal kingdom, even if there are a few examples, whereas coitus manifests itself in very diverse forms, including very long-lasting couplings. This leads us to consider, in his view, that jouissance, even in its purely organic form, cannot be reduced to the orgasm.[5]

This fundamental point of conjunction of biology with the unconscious subjectivity of one of the partners determines the limit of pleasure that by definition regulates the jouissance of each, in a way that is linked to the human specificity of inhabiting language. The law of the pleasure principle described by Freud, and undeniably verified since then, is the limit that subjectivity imposes on itself in order never to go beyond a certain threshold of pleasure, to avoid an anguishing jouissance which, at its most extreme, is deadly. This system of regulation, designed to maintain homoeostasis in the psychical apparatus, exists in all dimensions of pleasure and in all the drives, but the male orgasm is a prime example of it, because as a general rule it is the culmination of a jouissance as well as its end point. Lacan considered the orgasm to be the limit point of the subject, a place where every 'demand goes silent' or 'desire is tricked'. It is a moment of fleeting annihilation that 'represents the dimension of the subject in its tearing apart, in its division'.[6] It is triggered not by one's conscious will but by the subject of the unconscious, with very wide variations in the threshold of jouissance that is bearable; its modalities are entangled in the whole chain of desire and symptom that bind it together.

This point of unconscious subjectivity in the man is imposed on both partners as the limit of the sexual act, in the same way that erection opens up its possibility. It goes without saying that feminine subjectivity also has a limit in its relation to jouissance, but it does not manifest itself by making the sexual act biologically impossible, because the female body can always be penetrated. So we may suppose that the limit that is materialised, suspending the jouissance of both bodies in the sexual relation, constitutes a biological fact of the greatest importance, since it is taken up in language to form the basis of a logic. In the register of the drives, there is only one other case where the limit of pleasure of one body determines the limit for another, which is that of the mother for the child she carries and then feeds; and even this does not involve something of an involuntary biological nature.

The incidence of this particularity varies considerably according to the subjective position of the man in relation to jouissance, and especially to that of his partner. The impact the sexual law has on this is obvious, but it is also probable that it played a part in the construction of that very law. In all the great civilisations, and in all eras, the sexual laws regarding sexual relations have had one thing in common: the phallic function that defines the man as 'the one who has, and who has the one who is, the woman'. Just as the organ commands the jouissance of both, the phallus as sole signifier of jouissance elides that of the other.

The castration complex, with its many effects and functions in the unconscious, can now be understood in this light. The elements involved in the sexual encounter between man and woman are familiar in all discourses, but they had never been the subject of a psychoanalytic study on their impact in the unconscious. Whereas conversely, the effects of the unconscious on the unfolding of the sexual act, and its symptoms, have been well known since the discovery of psychoanalysis, and even before. Lacan completed his inaugural commentary by emphasising that the female orgasm was 'tubular by nature' – enigmatic and impossible to situate – though since then it has become far less so, and he pointed out that 'it's because man will never take the end point of his desire this far that we can say that his jouissance and that of the woman will not join organically'.[7] It is hard to imagine a better way of expressing the difficulty involved.

III. The phallic cut and the phantasy of a complementary object

The status of the phallic cut in the sexual relation is fundamental in the symbolic order. All human jouissances are subject to a limit, that of the pleasure principle, fixed at a greater or lesser distance by the subject of the unconscious, which is self-determined according to a range of factors, one of which is prohibition. The limit has an impact on the way the sexual relation unfolds, and consequently on how it is conceived of, if one can put it that way, since each partner ultimately finds that they are separated from their object of satisfaction, whether the separation is welcome or not. Certain logics of desire are constructed within language based on anatomical or physiological traits of the erogenous zones, which they interpret in a variety of ways. Here we are dealing not only with the colonisation of those zones by language, but also with logics borrowed from the biology of the zones to serve as a grammar in discourse.

These logics of the drives bring about the intervention of a bodily object: the breast, the buttocks, the erect penis, in the way it has been brought into play in a dialectic between this body and that of the other, and they define a relation of the subject to the Other according to the logic of one object or another. For example, the breast is a part of the mother, and yet the baby considers it to be part of its own body, so that at the time of weaning, it loses a part of itself. According to this oral logic, the organisation of desire would involve an object belonging to the Other, which the subject still considers belongs to themselves, and would consist in trying to take possession of it. This oral logic structures a variety of acts, for example, certain types of theft.

Conversely, for the child their stools or faeces are body parts, but with toilet training are subjected to the demand of the Other. The organisation of desire according to this anal logic therefore involves an object which belongs to the subject, and which has value only in so far as it is demanded by the Other, so that the subject has to yield it, but resists doing so because it is a part of themself.

The necessary separation of the subject from their object, through weaning and toilet training, causes a split in the primary unity of subjectivity, which Lacan condensed into the term 'separtition'.[8] Each stage of the formation of the subject involves their separation from an object and a splitting within themself. Each zone of the drives is therefore the site of the formation of a new object; this is triggered as much by language as by the body, resulting in a two-way interaction between them, and the subject maintains an intimate connection with the object, since it was a part of themself, and yet is external to them, since they are now separated from it. The loss of each object divides the subject, and makes them desire to refind those objects, since they were formerly part of themself.

This desire may be defined as autoerotic, since it does not aim at the field of the Other, but at a part of the subject.[9] It involves something unreal, phantasmatic, functioning as if empty, since it concerns a past object while addressing itself to one that is present. This is how the object of phantasy is constituted, and it may focus on someone without taking into account that they are a real person. This desire does not involve the field of the real Other, and thus it encounters a stumbling block where jouissance is concerned, which is in that field. In this sense, there is no promise of jouissance to the subject's desire, since desire concerns a part of themself, whereas jouissance is of the Other.

The object formed in the unconscious by the cut in the sexual relation, even though it is not formed in infancy, is based on the same logic. The detumescence that brings the sexual relation to an end produces the same status of lost object, separated from the subject and thus creating a division within them. The involuntary loss of erection that follows orgasm is a phallic loss in the sexual relation and causes the phantasy to emerge in the male subject of a lost object that has to be refound, like a part of himself that is lost, the lost phallus. This is how the phallic function is produced, and it is found again in the conditions of the sexual law.

The metaphor of Genesis also inaugurates a feminine object, and it does so through a comparable process: Eve is the result of a part of Adam that has been separated from him, extracted from him, and will be re-found in the form of a woman. In reality, this scenario is comparable in all its aspects with what occurs in each sexual act at the moment of its ending: a 'bone' is taken from the man, the bone of the erection that allows the sexual act to take place, and whose function is lost as if it were part of himself. He submits to this law of the pleasure principle as a limit, and brings it into operation as a divided subject of the unconscious. As Genesis so perfectly defines it, man is concerned with an object which occupies the function of the lost part of himself in his phantasy, the phallus which is extracted from him and which he aims to refind in his partner. This suggests that the same process is at work here, through its metaphorical evocation.

Furthermore, the scene from Genesis attributes the extraction of the organ to the Biblical God. The metaphor comprises God being named as the one who decides on the phallic cut in the sexual act, and creates a feminine object out of the lost phallus. Obviously this interpretation is based on the one made by Lacan, even though he hardly mentioned it, and we are now expanding on his idea.[10] We may wonder why an agent is attributed to this cut, since there is no need for one, and this is another question which is worth reflecting on.

This metaphor stems from the same structure as the one described as the paternal metaphor to account for the primary formation of the subject of the unconscious. In both cases, the agent of castration is a symbolic Father and the desire of the feminine Other is repressed in order that the phallic object, which desire aims at, can be substituted for it. The man is symbolically deprived of the phallus in infancy, in the sense that only the Father can have it, and this happens again at the limit of each sexual act in the sense that detumescence separates him from the functionality of his organ. The prospect of this cut brings about tension in the face of the other's call to jouissance, and constitutes a castration when the latter gets ahead of the cut or interrupts it. But it may also be experienced as a castration when the partner is satisfied, if the man feels himself to be an instrument of satisfaction, in the sense of being equivalent to the phallus rather than having it.

For a woman, this subtraction also has the value of castration if she has no jouissance. Her own desire is also orientated according to the 'biological rock'. She may either bring a feminine logic into play, which supplements the lack in the relation to the partner, or she may orientate herself, like the man, towards the desire for a new object, according to the same phallic jouissance. The subtraction plays the role of a determining cut in so far as the moment it occurs, it either follows or suspends the partner's jouissance. The whole concept of the sexual act is organised on this basis.

There is a fundamental dissymmetry in the biological facts of the sexual act: the possibility of the act, and then of its suspension, depend entirely on masculine biological determination, while the feminine side is presented as an availability at all levels. The female orgasm does not in any way interrupt the sexual act, and is capable of occurring multiple times, without intervening in the function of copulation other than from a subjective point of view. There are important consequences that can be deduced from the fact that the species of speaking beings is characterised by the male orgasm provoking an emission followed by the detumescence of the organ of copulation. This subtraction plays the part of a law regulating jouissance according to masculine subjectivity in its relation to the other. The subjective consequences of this are huge, but depend broadly on what the symbolic order currently in operation makes of it, for a particular subject in a given civilisation.

With this cut in functionality that physically brings about the limit of pleasure for both parties, the object of castration anxiety emerges from the closed field of autoerotism to confront the field of the Other. This is where castration finds its biological 'rock' – not in the form of an image of collapse or of a loss of the organ, but in the form of the subjective regulation of jouissance in the relation to the other. In this sense, a detumescent penis at the moment when two jouissances are articulated with one another does not have the effect of a castration, but simply of a welcome regulation, and this is true in masturbation as well.

The relation of the man to this cut in the functionality of his organ is so essential that it is the first object he has to deal with in the sexual relation, even before his partner. The man has to grapple with this phallus that is prone to being taken from him against his conscious will, and which in this sense functions as a third element in the couple.[11] Lacan went so far as to designate the phallus as the conscientious objection made by one of the two sexes to the service they were required to render to the other, and as an obstacle to the man's ability to have jouissance of the woman's body.[12] This remark concerns the particularities of the jouissance of the penis and its detumescence, as well as the signifier that has been constructed to determine subjective organisation and to form the sexual law. Its validity is greater at the level of subjectivity than at the biological level, because there are many types of unconscious modalities of objection of the phallic function to the jouissance of the other sex, in both senses of the genitive: objecting to the other's jouissance as well as to having jouissance of the other. As with all manifestations of the unconscious, they evolve according to the interpretations given to them, and according to the ambient ideological discourses. In our time, certain masculine sexual symptoms are on the increase, such as male anorgasmia, a symptom which is manifestly sensitive to a partner's expectation of fertilisation, or to the widespread media coverage in the last century devoted to premature ejaculation.

IV. Materialisation of the limit of pleasure through detumescence

This cutting of the sexual act, which obeys the pleasure principle and thus the unconscious limitation of jouissance by the subject, occurs when a certain threshold of jouissance is reached; this is highly variable, and where masculine physiology is concerned, it tends to be quite low, but it may also be brought forward or pushed back to an extreme degree by a variety of psychical factors, including those that are symptomatic. The withdrawal of penile functioning incarnates the limit of the pleasure principle, the unconscious law that governs the subject by drawing a line between pleasure and a jouissance that goes beyond it, which cannot be attained without paying the penalty of anxiety. The sexual cut is an exemplary illustration of the law of the pleasure principle, described by Freud in relation to all the drives, but it is only in the sexual drive that it is iso concrete.[13]

What is particular about this limit is that it imposes its law on both partners, since it entails the subtraction of jouissance for both rather than for one alone, whether it satisfies or not. Here we find the most fundamental definition of castration, represented as a subtraction at the level of the organ, whereas it is above all a subtraction of jouissance, due to the subtraction of the functionality of the organ. In the unconscious, the subtraction at the level of the organ becomes a metaphor for the subtraction of jouissance, since the former entails the latter, and it does not represent jouissance in any manner whatsoever. The former is substituted for the latter, which has a myriad of consequences, among which is the representation of that which consists in having jouissance sexually by that which consists in having jouissance from the organ, in the sense of its being available.

The sexual encounter is broadly orientated by this limit, which obeys the law of the pleasure of the male subject, divides him and makes his conjunction with the jouissance of the other a source of difficulty. The moment of the triggering of the limit takes on the appearance of a commandment[14]; it is by definition subject to unconscious regulation according to the pleasure principle, as is the erection that allows the sexual act to take place, in relation to the desire of the Other. The metaphor of Genesis gives an agent to this commandment, and the agent's name is God.

From all this, the phallic function, borrowed from the cut in the sexual act, retains only the erect penis and its detumescence as signifier of the jouissance of the sexual couple. It does not represent the relation in sexual terms, but in terms of one body having another at its disposal, defining one sex as the one that has, and the other sex as a complementary part of the former. And so the relation at stake in the law that derives from it consists for one sex in nothing more than making a representation of the jouissance of the other, or having jouissance of it, in the sense of having it at one's disposal.

This relation commingles the one flesh of the mythical couple of Genesis, constructed on the fact that one single jouissance operates in the limit of pleasure of the sexual act,[15] and that this limit is substituted for a conjunction of the two. The body and jouissances 'are made one' in a double sense, since the relation of one with the other as part of himself is substituted for the joining of two. In other words, the articulation of the sexes is divided in two.

V. Sexual grammar of discourse

Sexual laws are clearly based on this kind of concept, formed by the unconscious, and operating in the gap between the modes of bodily jouissance of the two sexes, and comes to represent the relation according to only one sex, so that in this sense it is no longer a sexual relation. By eliding the jouissance of the woman, just as the phallic cut does, by preceding it, the law substitute the feminine object for it in one way or another. In the Western world, the Judeo-Christian religions have added the signifier of an agent of the cut, and an author of the sexual law. And this signifier adds all its authority to sever the articulation of the two jouissances in favour of whatever allows fertilisation, to the detriment of jouissance, while conversely, the weight of this commandment at the core of every sexual act reinforces its authority, marked in each son through circumcision. The Biblical God, according to Freud's logic, restored all his rights to the primal Father.

The system of the Name of the Father is not solely responsible for the construction of this law. The symbolic phallic function, resulting from the facts of the biological 'rock', has itself given rise to comparable sexual laws. The uncertain conjunction of two jouissances has been elided in all cases, through the substitution of the relation of the one with the other as object of desire. Just as in a dream, this metaphorical operation proceeds according to a rebus that cuts into the non-conjunction of jouissances in order to substitute a relation that renounces any possible conjunction. It effectively creates a structure of the order of a phantasy, formed of a subject conjoined to his object as a part of himself. In some sense he espouses the material phallic cut as the limit of the relation. Just as the organ loses its functionality, whether or not the partner's orgasm has been attained, so the law of the relation between the sexes is organised according to phallic jouissance and its limits alone, eliding the question of the jouissance of the other sex. The way penile jouissance functions means it is susceptible to not allowing a bodily conjunction of the jouissances of the two sexes, and the functioning of the phallus in the unconscious and in the sexual law makes this fact even more radical, by not articulating two desires and two jouissances between the sexes. The law cuts into the difficulty in order to resolve it, like cutting the Gordian knot, substituting the availability of a body, in the sense of either having it or being it, for the conjunction of jouissances.

Formulated in this way, the relation between the sexes involves a phallic dialectic which is linked to the phallic dialectic of infancy. The agent of castration is a Father, since Father has become what names it, and so this logic maps very simply onto the logic that emerged from the Oedipus complex. The Father guarantees that the prohibition of incest shall be respected, by imposing a logic that excludes one from having the phallus at the same time as being it, while one has the other who is it; and the sexual law achieves the same result by quite other means. There is thus a convergence between what is organised around a feature of the sexual act and what is organised around the law of the Oedipal Father. We may wonder if this convergence occurs because one facet is the result of the other, or whether two different causes result in the same logic; we will return to this later.

The reason for a number of the characteristics of the logic of the phallic function can be found here. The function of the phallus in the unconscious has been omnipresent since the beginnings of psychoanalysis, and it is recognised by all as an obvious signification which appears everywhere in discourse, far beyond the psychoanalytic field. This swarming signification appears to be the result of a powerful system of metaphor, which links the entire phallic symbolism of the sexual relation with, or superimposes it on, the function of the Father as guarantor of the prohibition of incest. Although the signifier of the phallus is supposed to join the complementary desires of man and woman, it governs their jouissance with a failure of its function of mediation, so that both sexes are organised around this quality of failure or fading.

Lacan summarised this state of affairs by saying that the phallus functions everywhere except where you would expect to find it.[16] Each sex has a relation to the phallus without that meaning that they have a relation to each other, and the same goes for each partner in a sexual couple. The phallus is only apparently a symbolic mediator in the encounter between the sexes, proliferating in the imaginary in the same way; it is not a mediator of the conjunction of their jouissances, even less so as a signifier than as an organ, since it is through the phallus that the law renounces the organ. The signifier is borrowed from the functioning of an organ that gives up its functionality at the threshold of jouissance, and the logic that borrows it retains only the limit of phallic jouissance, as if there were no further question of serving the jouissance of the other.

The phallus is established as the logical copula everywhere except in the sexual relation, precisely because in the sexual relation it is not the logical copula. It is thus as a missing copula – incarnating the limit of pleasure for both sexes and not articulating their jouissance – that the phallus is established as a signifying instrument in a logic of the difference of the sexes and of their relation. On the basis of the functional subtraction that limits jouissance, it is established conversely as the symbol of power, and then as a signifier that cannot be negated. From then on it assumes the signification of plus and minus, with the presence and absence initially encountered in infancy in the discovery of the sexes, according to the context of the discourse in which the child is immersed. Lacan revisited the notion of *Penisneid* from this new perspective; up till then it had broadly been described in psychoanalysis as the woman's nostalgia for the penis when faced with an absence that was experienced as a castration. He considered that it was not a wish to possess the organ but rather a desire to do better than the phallus in the mediation of the two jouissances.[17]

The sexual relation of man and woman can therefore be considered as a conjunction in an impasse, which the unconscious does not represent as such but rather symbolises its function in a state of failure. On the basis of this 'biological rock', the unconscious constructs a symbol which inverts the lack of power, which is no longer a power to conjoin two jouissances, but rather that of a subject in the place of their object of phantasy. Over all, there is nothing to castrate, since the phallus is constructed for no reason other than to avoid anxiety, to deal with the gap in the articulation of the jouissances of the two sexes, by substituting the logic of one sole jouissance and its limit.[18] Castration anxiety is not primarily the risk of losing the symbol of power: that has always already been lost, since it is constructed in such a way as to palliate its own loss, in order to supplement the withdrawal of the copulatory function that leaves a gap open between the jouissances.

So we can isolate a natural law, the 'biological rock' that has always been visible, without any scientific advance being necessary in order to identify it. While being a biological law, it is also subject to infinite variations because it can be altered subjectively, since the limit of pleasure is susceptible to being brought forward or pushed back in individual cases. On the basis of a tendency to non-conjunction and of a subjectivisation of castration that is on the horizon, everything that is at stake for each partner in the sexual relation follows a pathway towards jouissance, with or without love, with or without desire, and with or without orgasm. The sexual law has substituted its universal sanction for a certain disjunction in the sexual relation, inscribing in it a relation that concerns only one jouissance and its object. One jouissance is elided, or even proscribed in discourse, and thus has greater subjective difficulty in occurring, whereas a jouissance that is prescribed can occur far more rapidly.

So from this perspective, we can see that sexual law, which appears simply to echo the organic difficulty of conjunction, in fact also radicalises it, since it ignores the jouissance that is difficult to access, and which is not necessary to the process of fertilisation. The law elides the latter jouissance, giving up on articulating the jouissance of one sex with that of the other, and by converting this difficulty into an absence, it empties the place of the other sex in discourse, turning her into merely an object of discourse. It constructs a norm with the value of a logical schema, where one sex makes use of the other like a part of itself. There is truly an interpretative metaphor here! This elaboration of the sexual law is a solution substituted for a primary gap, and it has the advantage of logical facility in terms of discourse, but it engenders a number of impasses.

The symbolic organisation of the relation of man to woman does not articulate two signifiers any more than it does two jouissances, since it is organised around one phallic signifier which is both the cause of a gap and the solution it proposes to the cut that has left the sexes exiled from one another. Beyond symbolic castration, which psychoanalysis has recognised in terms of a possible or actual lack of the phallus in the subjective construction of sexuation, we can see the rock of the castration complex revealed, which is at the heart of the sexual relation: this concrete limit to pleasure when one is faced with the other's call to jouissance.

Notes

1 Paul Verhaeghe, *Love in a Time of Loneliness,* London, Routledge, 2011, p. 5.
2 Sigmund Freud, *Analysis Terminable and Interminable*, Standard Edition, 23, London, Hogarth, 1964, p. 252.
3 Lacan, *Anxiety*, op. cit., p. 238.
4 Lacan, *Anxiety*, op. cit., pp. 263–4, translation modified.
5 Jacques Lacan, *The Object of Psychoanalysis*, seminar of 27 April 1966.
6 Ibid.
7 Lacan, *Anxiety*, op. cit., p. 265, translation modified.

8 Ibid., p. 237.
9 This is how Lacan defined it: 'Desire functions inside a world which, however shattered, carries the trace of this original closing off inside what remains of the envelope of the egg, whether this is imaginary or virtual'. Ibid., translation modified.
10 This interpretation is found in the fragment referred to earlier: 'When I say that it's in the object a that the sexual partner will always necessarily be refound, we see the truth inscribed in Genesis'. Jacques Lacan, *The Psychoanalytic Act*, seminar of 21 February 1968. But also, he adds later on: 'This rut of the Name of the Father, of the father who names that appears in the Bible . . . is for the man a way of removing his phallus from the game'. 'This tribal God is just the useless complement . . . who gives to the asexual body of the man his missing partner. Missing in what way? Because he is "aphlicted" with a phallus which is what blocks the jouissance of the body of the Other'. Jacques Lacan, *RSI*, seminar of 11 March 1975.
11 Lacan emphasises this, for example: 'if there is a moment when the man can lose sight of the presence of the third term, it's in the fleeting moment where he loses, because he weakens, what is not only his instrument, but for both him and the woman, the third term in the relation of the couple'. Jacques Lacan, *Logic of the Phantasy*, seminar of 1 March 1967.
12 'Analytic discourse shows, if you'll allow me to out it like this, that the phallus, is the conscientious objection made by one of two sexed beings to the service to be rendered to the other. . . . I'll go further, phallic jouissance is the obstacle by which man fails to enjoy the woman's body, precisely because what he enjoys is the enjoyment of his organ'. Jacques Lacan, *Encore,* The Seminar Book 20, ed. J-A Miller, New York, Norton, 1998, p. 7, translation modified.
13 Lacan refers to it thus: 'Detumescence in the genital act, being the characteristic of the penile organ, is precisely the fact that it keeps jouissance in suspense, and introduces this: that there is a jouissance beyond it'. Jacques Lacan, *Logic of the Phantasy*, seminar of 24 May 1967.
14 Let us recall how Lacan described this: 'The other pole of the signifier, its stopping action, is also there at the origin of the vocative of commandments'. Lacan, *Encore*, op. cit., p. 24. A man can evoke it by asking himself, 'Where does that order come from?'
15 The Christian meaning of 'one flesh' gives its literal weight to this metaphorical formation of the biblical woman.
16 *Anxiety*, op. cit., p. 219.
17 Lacan, *Anxiety*, op. cit., p. 259.
18 'The fact that the phallus is not to be found where it's expected, where it's demanded, namely, on the plane of genital mediation, is what explains how anxiety is the truth of sexuality, that is, what appears each time its tide washes back to reveal the sand beneath. Castration is the price of this structure, it comes into the place of this truth. But in fact, this is illusory. There is no castration because, in the place where it is supposed to occur, there is no object to castrate. The phallus would have to have been there for that, but it is in fact only there to get rid of anxiety'. Ibid., p. 269, translation modified.

Chapter 3

Deconstruction of the sexual law

I. Castration in childhood and in the sexual relation

In childhood, castration is structured around the desire of the mother, for whom the child wishes to be the phallic object she desires, and then around the intervention of the father or a third party, in the name of a Father who alone is in command of the phallus and is the one who possesses it. Therefore the child has no way of remaining identified with the phallus for the mother, let alone of having it. This castration spares the child from becoming alienated in the relation to the mother centred on the object of desire. This logical process, which forms the basis of unconscious subjective structuration, constitutes the system that organises the key points of sexuation. Since the Name of the Father, the religious and social keystone of this construction, has become far less widespread as a belief, the sequence of events that constructs desire has evolved, and it is now established differently. And it is clear that there is absolutely no necessity for a single agency to guarantee that all the paternal functions are put into place; this can be done just as well by a variety of agencies.

In the sexual relation, castration takes on an additional meaning, and both its causes and its effects are distributed in a different way. Each individual approaches it according to the symbolic order imparted by their parental and social Other, according to the position they have taken up in it, but then when they enter the field of the actual sexual relation, another unconscious determination will come into play in their relation to the Other, superimposed onto the structures laid down in childhood.

The castration complex is formed by the unconscious on the basis of an element that is not included in childhood itself: the sexual relation of man and woman. Each civilisation, in interpreting the particularity of sexual jouissance in the relation between the two sexes, deduces from it a sexual law with its symbols, signifiers and rules of jouissance. Although there is enormous diversity, and a variety of developments have taken place in different geographical areas and different epochs, these laws display a common orientation based not on the union of two, but on the one and his object as part of himself, which is parallel to the fact that

DOI: 10.4324/9781003285984-4

the cut in jouissance produced in the one has its effect on both parties. For both parties, the grammar of the discourse of the law is constructed like a phallic function based on this cut.

It suffices, then, that its agent is a Father in order for it to connect with the phallic logic of childhood, and that in both cases he commands castration to be carried out. In the sexual law, the Biblical God operates in a way that is comparable to that of the Oedipal Father, who forbids the jouissance of the mother – in both its genitive meanings – and substitutes the function of object for that jouissance. The Father is inaugurated as an agent of castration in both these major aspects of subjectivity, one at the heart of the formation of a subject in childhood, and the other at the heart of the organisation of a relation between the sexes within the social bond. Lack is distributed differently in the one and the other castration. In the discourse of the law, each party has a relation to the phallus, without that creating a relation between them, and the lack is placed unilaterally on the side of the woman, making her the object of desire, in order to base one party's having on the lack in the other.

In the real of the sexual relation, the lack is shared, due to the failure of the phallus to conjoin the jouissances when confronted with the underlying biological laws and their subjective inflexions. The biological failing of orgasms to coincide involves two 'failures', since the tardiness of the one compounds the detumescent hastiness of the other. The coincidence of jouissances also clashes with the sexual grammar of discourse, in which the sexuated relation concerns only the phantasy of one sex, and elides the desire of the other. The phallus, so important in the representation of both male and female sexuality, is never to be found where it is hoped for as a mediation between the desires and the jouissances of the two sexes.[1]

So it is not there to articulate them but for some other reason. The sexual law based on the phallic function is constructed with other aims than that of conjoining two sexes. It is not created to unite them – although that is not to say that it is intended not to unite them – but what goes into the construction of the sexual law concerns something else. It cuts into the gap in the conjunction of two jouissances, making it even more radical, and yet it presents itself as a solution to the gap that is already there. So although it fails to articulate a 'sexual relation' between man and woman, the sexual law has the function of making up for its deficiencies. We can no longer consider that the disjunction of the jouissances of man and woman is nothing more than an effect of discourse and the sexual law. Nor can we continue to simply think that this law, based on the phallic function, consists merely in applying the structures derived from the prohibition of incest, through having created a distance between the man's desire and anything that might evoke the jouissance of the mother.

So here we have the introduction, the discovery, of a vast supplementary dimension of psychoanalytic thinking that extends the foundations of its theory. The castration complex is now seen to be based on and explained by this sort of unconscious commandment, which to the man seems to come from somewhere else, from a God, to trigger the climax of pleasure and its limit, while at the same time it creates a gap, heavily laden with consequences, between his sex and the other sex.

Two very distinct sources, initially appearing to be quite disproportionate, seem to feed into a single symbolic and logical order, to form what the subject of language, of the unconscious, has to deal with. The borrowed material is added to that which was excluded in order to create the fundamental signifiers of the subject's discourse. According to Freud's experience, psychoanalysis was born out of the discovery of the incestuous phantasy, with its virtually eternal influence on subjectivity and sexuality. In 1963, another dimension was opened up, when Lacan's research led him to discover a second fundamental aetiology, based on the 'biological rock' of castration, from which he later deduced the absence of the 'sexual relation' with its effects, which are also eternal, on subjectivity and sexuality.

II. The feminine object produced by the phallic cut

As told in Genesis, the sexual law is the foundation for one flesh, according to the articulation of one who has and one who is. This singular connection of a subject with an object that is a part of him, his other half, as we say, involves only one desire and is supported by a single symbol. It is structured like a phantasy, and certainly organises nicely the idea of making One in the sexual act, but in quite another way than what would consist in conjoining two jouissances. It involves a relation of 'one plus a' and not of two ones, since the object a does not count as one. Although within the terms of this description, there is considerable latitude for the organisation of feminine desire, we are well aware of the serious consequences it has had, and as our societies have developed, there is now a refusal to buy into this grammar as a unique law imposed on everyone.

What is more, the law does not exactly deal with jouissance as such, but establishes that one body is deemed to have the other at its disposal, substituting 'having jouissance of' for 'having jouissance'. So here we can see a displacement. The metaphor of Genesis speaks only of a sleeping man, and of the extraction of a part of his body giving form to another body; there is no longer any question of jouissance. The law annuls jouissance and replaces it by the belonging of one body to another. There is nothing specifically sexual about this, but it forms the basis for a pairing of the bodies of the two sexes which makes sense according to a symbolic relation of a subject and its object.

So the symbolisation of sex in psychical life has been replaced by something that is not sexual, and this has been noted in our time, with all its consequences. The function of woman as phallus-object is central to the logic of this discourse, which has given up trying to establish a relation between the two, where both jouissances and subjectivities are concerned. Where each subject is concerned, the law's prescription has linked up with what was induced by the Oedipal system of the Name of the Father when the prohibition of incest was in full force, in the logical alternative between having or being the phallic object. And since it appears that the creation of the concept of the phallus in the unconscious, even right from the beginning, stems from a logic borrowing a trait from the sexual relation, the creation of the feminine object as the imaginary equivalent of the phallus must stem from the same source. Let us see how this happens.

Following Freud's theorisation, psychoanalysis considered that object libido was formed by a transfusion based on ego libido. Since the ego is diminished when it loves, it seemed that it had borrowed capital from the libido in order to invest in the object. Primary narcissism, once it had been formed, remained only to be taken out, like Adam's rib, to be transfused into the formation of Eve. Simple reasoning, perhaps, but quite false, since it is based on a phantasy. The notion of the gift of the phallus in the sexual act, which shares the same principle of oblation considered as a sign of genital maturity, was first criticised by Lacan in the light of what actually occurs in sexual jouissance. For him it was nothing short of comical to consider that it was a gift, when it was quite obvious that there was a complete failure here in the conjunction of jouissances.

In reality, woman is constituted as object of desire and of jouissance according to an inverse process, which goes from a minus to a plus, and not from a plus to a minus. The loss of phallic functionality divides the subject in himself, causing the emergence of a phantasy of an object to be refound as a part of himself. It is absolutely not the case of a narcissism pouring itself into an object, but on the contrary, of a lack opened up by the phallic cut, which impels the subject to refind an object that takes on the value of what has been lost.

The phallic cut in the sexual relation constitutes the loss of an object that is at the heart of the subject, and is the very model of the object formed on the basis of a physiological separation which is appropriated by language, and which Lacan named *a*, the small other (*autre*) reduced to a letter. As is the case for all objects of the drives, this separation satisfies the regulation of the pleasure principle that the subject of the unconscious maintains according to a higher or lower threshold in the relation to jouissance and to the jouissance of the other. The subtraction of jouissance is therefore masked, except in cases of premature ejaculation, in other words, of premature detumescence.[2]

However, the jouissance subtracted is still 'counted' in the unconscious, where everything that has been lost must be refound in any form whatsoever to take its place. It is therefore carried over, displaced elsewhere, later on, in a different form. This is the process that causes desire: the very wellspring of desire, in all the drives, the demand, the impulse that consists in wanting to, having to recuperate what has been taken away or lost, in whatever form possible, in order for that thing to take its place and stop the gap and mend the division caused by the loss. That is how desire is caused, depending on the different forms of object that emerge from the cut and the separation, but it is particularly notable for a number or reasons in the case of the sexual relation.

Indeed, in the case of the sexual relation this process contributes to the formation of a logic that will operate everywhere else as well, because it is borrowed to form the basis of a symbolic system and an economy. The basis of the economy is first of all the annulment of the jouissance subtracted, and its transformation into the value of jouissance, a value which functions in the same way as what Marx called exchange value. Annulling jouissance as such consists in not taking into account the fact that it has been subtracted, in wiping out the loss by establishing a value that conceals a promise of jouissance that appears to be the same, but in fact is different. The jouissance deducted from the phallic organ through the cut in the sexual relation is annulled because its subtraction satisfies the pleasure principle, but it is *carried forward* as object libido in order to constitute the woman as the phallic object. In this process the woman represents a value of jouissance which from then on is equivalent to an exchange value.[3]

A process of this nature corresponds in all points to what we have observed regarding the structure of the sexual law. So that we may suppose that what is valid for the subject of phallic jouissance was also borrowed for the elaboration of the discourses and laws organising the relation of the sexes in civilisations, because it constitutes the pivot of a fundamental articulation. This process comprises an annulment of the subtraction, its repression, and the formation of a phantasy concerning the partner of the other sex. This articulation distributes jouissance, or whatever takes its place, and forms the basis for the relation between the subject who has (use value) and the other who is (exchange value). Established as a sexual law, it constitutes the sexuated relation expressed as the social bond between man and woman. Lacan designated the phallic jouissance subtracted from the man according to the pleasure principle as the 'insertion point necessary for any sexual ideology'.[4] His reading and critique of this sexual ideology is both enlightening and persuasive.

This source of sexual ideology is based on the limit of masculine jouissance in the sexual relation, using it to create a law. The knot of jouissance and subtraction, in relation to the call of the jouissance of the other, is the foundation of the concept of the phallus. Castration comes to symbolise the subtraction, and through the reversal of the minus into a plus, of the loss into a power, it forms the phallus.[5] And this can function either as a symbol that wards it off and overcomes it, or as a signifier that annuls it.

One might think that the formation of the concept of the phallus, from ancient times onwards, would have involved a certain knowledge that the functioning of penile jouissance satisfied the aim of fertilisation rather than of jouissance itself. So that the phallic function of the law makes a precise choice by symbolising what is necessary for the emission of semen, and by eliding whatever is not necessary for procreation, even though over a long period of time the belief prevailed in many discourses that the female orgasm was necessary in order to procreate. The signifier of the sexuated relation of the law picked up on this trend in the sexual relation that satisfied the aim of procreation while giving up on jouissance as such, as the latter would have entailed conjoining the two. The law that symbolically cuts into the conjunction of jouissances, and therefore of the sexes, excludes the dimension of jouissance from the sexual relation in favour of the aim of procreation. So the phallus, created in this way as a signifier that concerns only one jouissance, is thus the only signifier for both sexes, as it is also the only signifier to symbolise the desire of the mother.

We can observe the reversal that operates if things are considered in this way. The woman, as phallic object, is certainly a part of the man in this sense, just as she was in the metaphor of Genesis. But contrary to the metaphor, she is not derived from the man's point of view from a 'plus' that tends towards becoming a 'minus', but from a 'minus' that insists on recuperating a 'plus'. From this subtraction and the way it is carried forward, the idea arises of having jouissance of the feminine object, as from a lost part of himself. What seems to become 'transfused' from the man to the woman taken as object of desire, is the object that needs to be refound in order to compensate for the subtraction of the sexual act.

In the exchange of love, the object of desire seems always to have been recognised. This is an effect of the phantasy projected onto the other, the imaginary object of desire constructed on the basis of lost phallic jouissance. Constructed in this way, the woman is a feminine version of the man, the imaginary equivalent of the phallus. If she adheres to this position conferred on her by the law, she participates in a relation not of two, but of one alone based on subtraction. The object resulting from the subtraction does not involve the woman as such, and Lacan emphasised that she is capable of escaping from this ideological trap by situating herself beyond the phallic function of the law. It is only recently that this refusal of the law has met with a measure of success, since the woman has been able, silently, to develop another position outside discourse.

Since the metaphor of Genesis deals with the difficult conjunction of the sexes in terms of jouissance by eliding one of them, it demonstrates that the difficulty has actually been recognised. The sexes certainly do not form 'one flesh' in terms of jouissance, but another way of creating 'one flesh' is to have one body symbolically emerge from the other. The entire creation of the phallic signifier which in turn organised the sexuated relation of the law is condensed in this metaphor that elides the woman's jouissance by constituting her as an object.

The first God of monotheism is the agent of subtraction of a body part from the man, which is a metaphor for the subtraction of the erection that brings the sexual relation to an end. This God is invoked as being the one who decides to make the orgasm concomitant with ejaculation, which brings about detumescence. It is he who has control over the phallus and its withdrawal, who imposes this suspension of jouissance on both man and woman. Here we find the matrix of a symbolic order according to the logical principle of a cut between the sexes that is implied by the phallic function, which does not include any articulation of the two. The Name of the Father, like the phallus that becomes its instrument, symbolises a type of relation between man and woman that is based on a commandment for a subtraction rather than a conjunction, and thus masks the absence of the latter. Having been put in place as the being responsible for a symbolic phallic function that does not enable communication between two jouissances or two signifiers, and which, if unmitigated by any other influence, constitutes an obstacle to the relation between the two, he reinforces its traits. In command of the negative of the phallus as well as the positive, he secures them to each other like the two sides of a fabric, in one signifier he himself cannot negate, since he is its guarantor.

III. Autoerotism of phallic jouissance

A jouissance that involves nothing other than a part of the subject himself that has been cut off, and which he has to refind, has the characteristics of autoerotism even in the sexual relation, and even if it appears to involve another body by being projected onto it. The subject of the phallic function comes to the sexual act driven by this sole jouissance, which is not designed to articulate the sexual couple, but simply to deploy its own logic. The phallic mode of forming the feminine object, by carrying forward the jouissance that has been subtracted, constitutes a grammar capable of supporting a system of logic; that is its power. But it does not predispose to a jouissance that communicates with that of the other; something else has to intervene for that to happen. At first glance, a jouissance that is symbolised only on the basis of subtraction cannot be articulated with that of the other sex. This entire process forms the logical basis of a discourse, but it does not really symbolise the relation of one sex to another. One single substance forms its grammar, which concerns only the subject and the phallus, from the subtraction of jouissance to the formation of the phantasy of the object.

Desire caused in this way can only involve the partner through displacement. The cut and the loss of jouissance are the only factors causing a desire of this nature, and only the carrying over of the value of jouissance can incarnate it, as a 'plus' expected to compensate for the 'minus' of what has been subtracted. So this value that has already been established is imposed on the object that has been found, and it has little to do with the intrinsic being of the latter. This is the very process of phantasy, which creates an unreal object and projects it onto the other, without taking into consideration the true nature of that other. Phantasy moves towards an object that seems to be what desire is aiming at, whereas it is simply the one onto which the value of the loss that causes desire can be carried over. The neurotic subject is particularly vulnerable to this process, and it hinders access to what is real in a relation.

When this mode of jouissance is the only one operative, it is often actually autoerotic, and involves a difficulty in allowing the desire of the other to be included, because there is no place for it in this system. If the system remains entirely unchanged – if real encounters leave the logic of the phallic function intact – it means there is a very limited choice. The only options are either to persist in orientating oneself in the sexual act according to one's own jouissance, eliding that of the other, or, conversely, to put oneself completely at the service of the jouissance of the other, sacrificing one's own. The phallic function on its own consists of only one logic, that of the phallic 'all or nothing', and that would not be sufficient to find a pathway to the articulation with the jouissance of the other.

Lacan emphasised the autoerotic aspect of phallic jouissance, where there is only one subject involved, even in the relation between two.[6] He showed how this is conditioned by the subject representing the object of phantasy, constituting this value of jouissance as something refound, compensating for the loss. One such condition is being able to represent a form of castration, because the desire at stake in the phallic function aims at the lack in the other. According to Lacan, masculine desire involves a search to produce a lack in the woman that concerns only him;[7] the lack in her is situated at another level. Here he introduced a point of view that was radically new to psychoanalysis, along with a critique of the expectations of the sexual law and its phallic function, marking an essential difference from the psychoanalytic beliefs current at the time.

It was only much later that he would argue that, beyond the possibility of a specifically feminine jouissance in the relation to a man, a woman could also participate equally in phallic jouissance. And certainly, this jouissance of the subject in the woman's case is just as autoerotic as it is in the man's, coming in the same way from the carrying over of a portion of the jouissance that has been subtracted, in one way or another, onto an object constituted as a part of the subject. This is what is at stake in motherhood, where the child constitutes an object of this order, as part of the mother as subject. But it can also be deployed in the sexual relation in a masculine way, giving rise to orgasm in this case. It is not only linked to the clitoral jouissance of childhood, but also to the jouissance of all the subsequent phallic objects. It is at stake in everything that consists in speaking and continuing to speak, because it is closely linked to the phallus as the signifying basis of the order of discourse. Beyond motherhood and autoerotic sexuality, it has become more widespread since our civilisation has recognised women's capacity in professional or personal situations to speak up in whatever form. So that the autoeroticism of phallic jouissance is not simply the prerogative of men. The castration that is derived from it is at work in a comparable way as soon as one speaks, as soon as the object is cut off from the subject, masculine or feminine, inflicting on them the loss of a part of themselves, and causing in them the desire to refind an object to take its place.

IV. From 'jouissance' to 'jouissance of'

Having jouissance *of* something is different from having jouissance. In this case, the jouissance at stake is replaced by the notion of having something at one's disposal, in the same way that, in the legal sense, to have the usufruct of property means to have it at one's disposal, sometimes without actually possessing it. The sexual law never mentions a sexual jouissance, but only what consists in having something at one's disposal. Being the one (masculine) who has, and having the one (feminine) who is, is not equivalent to jouissance; there is a displacement involved. It is activated in the same way as phallic jouissance. And something stops the man from having jouissance of the body of the woman as such.

The mode of jouissance of the penis, involving the loss of functionality that is always on the horizon, is what prevents this jouissance, it prevents the man from having jouissance of the other as body, because it is tied to the limit of jouissance of his own organ, in the same way as it is tied to the signifier that governs its functioning. Having a relation to this mode of jouissance that entails its own limit regulated by the subject of the unconscious, or even by a symptom, takes precedence over the reality of the partner. What is more, the subtraction of jouissance that marks this limit is annulled and transformed into a value, and jouissance itself is annulled and then displaced onto having a body at one's disposal, which brings with it the idea of having jouissance of it, whereas it is precisely there that it has been renounced. 'Having jouissance of' does not involve a jouissance of the body but having it at one's disposal,[8] which, as in its legal usage, entails the renunciation of a jouissance. One only has this body at one's disposal if jouissance is displaced, if it is no longer a jouissance, indeed it never was one, since it is barred by phallic subtraction. The so-called complementary relation of having and being, between man and woman, articulates a 'having jouissance of' rather that a jouissance.[9]

The law of kinship and exchange which remained in force for centuries has the same roots as the sexual law, and is based on the displacement that annuls jouissance and elides it. The insistence on virginity expresses this annulment, since the act of deflowering puts the emphasis on the fact of being the first to have the other's body at one's disposal – in the way one might break the seal of a letter – rather than on having jouissance with it.

Lacan analysed an analogous displacement in the dialectic of master and slave; not that one can compare that with the relation of man and woman in our time, in the West, but because we can observe in it the same type of renunciation of jouissance. It differs from Hegel's analysis, in which he proposed that the master has jouissance because he risked his life for it, whereas the slave does not have jouissance because he did not do so; he describes having a body at one's disposal, but not a jouissance. Instead of having jouissance, the master has the body of the slave at his disposal; the latter loses the right to disposal of his own body, but retains jouissance of his objects such as the look and the voice, and even sexual jouissance.

Similarly, the man under the aegis of the sexual law has renounced jouissance by displacing it onto the woman's body, which becomes a metaphor of his jouissance while eliding hers. When a mode of jouissance is operating that stems from the carrying forward of the value of this jouissance, of this logic of the phantasy that links the subject to the object as a part of himself, there is no question of knowing whether the object itself has jouissance, except via having this value for the other. The sexual law is constituted through an unconscious phantasy based on the carrying forward of a phallic jouissance that has been subtracted, where jouissance itself is annulled and displaced, making it into a 'jouissance of' the woman, having her at one's disposal as a value of jouissance. This sums up all that is present in the inscription of the relation of man and woman. So it is neither a jouissance as such nor a relation of two sexes, a 'sexual relation' in this sense. In discourse, there is nothing capable of symbolising this relation.

The unconscious created this grammar of discourse based on the limit point of masculine jouissance, and thus constituted a powerful root for the logos. The jouissance symbolised by castration and its inversion into power has the closest possible links with discourse. Here, value takes the place of jouissance and has as its sole signification the phallus, which is substituted everywhere for the jouissance that is annulled. Ancient Greece, the civilisation of the logos *par excellence*, was also the one that invented the concept of the phallus.

The disjunction of jouissances in the sexual relation is thus broadly accentuated by the terms of the law of the relation between the sexes. The phallic function constitutes an obstacle to the relation of the two, by not involving the jouissance of the woman as such, and reducing that of the man to having her at his disposal as a part of himself. In this sense, the phallus is the only One, at the level of jouissance, and Lacan made a joke of it: 'it is only the phallus that is happy – not the bearer of said. Even when, not out of oblation, but out of desperation, he places it, the said phallus, inside a partner, who is supposedly upset at not being its bearer herself'.[10] Here he was pursuing his ironical critique of a psychoanalytic concept that was very much alive at the time, the phantasy of the oblation of the man who was supposed to give the phallus in the sexual act, whereas in fact something quite different takes place.

This notion of oblation, deemed to be a sign of genital maturity according to the common beliefs of the time, is exposed here as exactly what it really is – a phantasy, generally an obsessional one, complemented by a seeking out, which could be considered sadistic, of the lack in the woman. As its corollary it attributes a *Penisneid* to the woman, a wish to possess the penis, without any relation to the reality of feminine desire, but only to symptomatic cases. The idea of a gift made in the sexual act to the partner who has no penis by the one who has it, has nothing at all to do with the reality of sexual jouissance. It is in fact an imaginary effect of the process of the annulment of subtraction and aims to carry it forward as a value. This phantasy reverses the flow as if a plus is given to a minus. The plus seems to pour itself into the minus, like a communicating vase, whereas it is first of all a minus that aims to be completed by a plus. This is why masculine desire aims to hollow out a lack in the other.

However, in hysterical neurosis, the absence of the organ is really considered by the subject to be a castration, and the castration is repressed. The logic of this neurosis is formed in the opposite way to the sexual law. Judging the latter to be flawed, the subject refuses it for themself, while signing up to it for the other. While the law makes castration unilateral on the side of the woman, the hysteric inverts this proposition by mirroring it, making it unilateral on the side of the man, and this is why there is also a discourse of the hysteric.

The sexuated relation set out in the law is thus both a cause of the absence of the articulation of the two sexes in a discourse, and one solution to their lack of sexual conjunction. It aims to symbolise a way of relating between them, and to inscribe them as a sexuated couple. The price paid for that, and which our civilisation has decided not to pay for the last half century, is not so much the annulation of jouissance, which in any case takes place in discourse. Apart from the subjugation of woman in the social bond, which has nowadays been rejected, it is more the radicalisation of the non-relation of the sexes involved in the phallic function, since it only involves one of them. This, we are told, is what Lacan said on the subject of Genesis: 'that's why things have gone so badly since then regarding the perfection that is imagined to be the conjunction of two jouissances',[11] at the same time as he declared that our civilisation was no longer prepared to pay the price.

However, this law leaves a degree of freedom to construct, for those who wish to do so, what can be considered a real 'sexual relation' outside of the law's discourse, if by that we understand something that links two partners of the two sexes, and consists in articulating their desires and their jouissances. We can certainly speak of a sexual relation in another sense in a couple of the same sex, but in the everyday sense, rather than in a Lacanian sense, since what he contested was precisely there being a possible relation between two sexes.

V. 'Having jouissance of' or 'making the other have jouissance': two phallic modes of jouissance

We know from experience the distinct modalities of masculine phallic jouissance determined by the phallus. They are illustrated in the literature on famous seducers, who are schematically divided into two groups: those who devote themselves to having jouissance of women, and those who cause them to have jouissance. Don Juan, a mythical character, is generally placed in the former category, while Casanova, who was a real person, even if the story of his life reads more like a novel, is to be found in the latter. It is easy to distinguish the logic of the former, consisting in seducing women while taking them away from another man or from a father, which is in opposition to the law of the phallic function, while retaining the same logic. The second logic consists in offering oneself up to their desire and serving their jouissance, and so does not entirely subscribe to the phallic function. One might initially think that one implies the other, and that they work on an equal footing. However, their logics are quite distinct from one other, and they do not bring into play the same register of the phallus, even if they both involve it. They can be explained by making a distinction between two modalities of the relation to jouissance.

In one case, jouissance is aimed at as such, based on that of the other, and the phallus is the symbol of what can overcome the obstacle in order to obtain it. The symbol is not cut off from jouissance, which is an integral part of what it symbolises. The phallic symbol of the Ancient Greeks can be found on every street corner, according to the multiple significations of its power, in terms of fertility, jouissance or even hospitality. In the other case, it is not a question of achieving jouissance, but of having the other at one's disposal. Here, the signifier is cut off from jouissance. Neither the image of the phallus nor that of the object play any part in it whatsoever. The signifier no longer concerns what causes jouissance, but rather what consists in having jouissance of, in the sense of being the master of it, and for the woman this means making herself the signifier of jouissance of the other, without herself having jouissance of it.

There is a considerable difference between these two symbolic modalities. The second modality, involving the signifier, undergoes an extra twist in symbolisation, which includes a renunciation of jouissance, its annulment and displacement, accompanied by the disappearance of its representation. The first modality, the symbol, functions quite differently, because as is the case in contemporary discourse, it is that of desire and of power, and aims to cause jouissance in the other rather than having the other at its disposal. It is the symbol of the jouissance of the woman, in the sense that she has jouissance of it, while the phallic signifier is that of the jouissance of the woman in the sense of jouissance being had of her; the genitives are not the same. When the phallus functions as a symbol, it does not stand in the way of the relation, and it tends to reduce the gap between the jouissances of man and woman. The signifier in no way reduces the gap, but rather increases it, but at the same times masks it by substituting the scenario in which one body has the other at its disposal. On the side of the symbol, there are men who cannot bear it if the woman does not have jouissance; on the side of the signifier, there are others who cannot bear it if she does. In the same way, there are women who cannot bear not to have jouissance, and others who cannot bear to.

When a woman has jouissance, whether or not she has an orgasm, she attributes the phallus as symbol to the man who arouses the jouissance. The phallus as symbol bears witness to the fact that the difficulty in conjoining their jouissances has been identified and overcome, and that the limit of jouissance has been recognised and surmounted. It results from the woman's jouissance, and similarly, it has a link with the imaginary and the real. It does not feature at all in the sexual law, since in that law jouissance is annulled and the woman's jouissance is passed over in silence; but in contemporary discourse the phallus as symbol is present everywhere, in the imaginary and in dreams.

The sexual law stems from the phallic signifier, not from the phallic symbol. The 'complementary' relation that it enshrines involves the phallus's belonging to one sex as an *a priori*, a given, by conflating it with the organ. It is based on the man's phallic jouissance, and does not borrow a single trait from the woman's jouissance, since the latter is elided. It annuls the limit of phallic jouissance, masking it and repressing it, whereas the imaginary phallus overcomes it and surmounts it. Where the signifier elides the jouissance of the woman, the symbol seeks it out. The signifier, a universal characteristic attributed in the name of the Father to one sex, radicalises the non-relation between the sexes while at the same time masking it. It reclaims the autoerotic dimension from phallic jouissance, with the same consequences in the symbolic order, namely to ignore the two of sex. The only remaining possibility for the functioning of the phallic symbol of feminine jouissance is to be found in the gaps in signification.

Different effects, in different registers, are produced on the basis of a similar disjunction at the heart of the sexual relation, on the basis of a similar cut. The sexual law masks, but at the same time intensifies, the disjunction between the sexes, by substituting the notion of the complementarity of subject with its object. The functioning of the phallic symbol reduces the disjunction, and in the imaginary register objects to the effects of the signifier, while having effects in the real. It is what a woman appeals to, it is what she desires in order to develop her jouissance. 'She has jouissance' forms the basis for 'he has it'. Within this framework, masculine phallic jouissance is articulated with that of the particular woman, and is not autoerotic; this is its singular, rather than universal, point of junction with feminine jouissance.

In reality, these two processes cohabit or succeed each other in a variable way, but one necessarily takes precedence over the other, with quite distinct effects. A psychoanalysis that has reached its conclusion will have reduced the function of the phallic signifier and that of the universal law, in order to allow a form of relation that is invented case by case.

VI. Subtraction of jouissance and feminine desire

The effects of the subtraction of jouissance as the limit of pleasure in the sexual relation primarily stem from the fact that the limit depends on masculine subjectivity. It is initially on the side of the man that it is inscribed in castration and causes the formation of a phantasy object that fills the gap of the loss, since it is subtracted from his jouissance. However, the effect of this cut has a similar impact on the side of the woman, and she orientates herself in her desire and her jouissance on the basis of something which for her too presents itself as a castration. Of course the final detumescence only constitutes a castration for her to a very variable degree, depending on whether she has experienced a form of jouissance or not, whether or not accompanied by orgasm. Lacan commented:

> In other words, the fact that male desire meets its downfall before entering the jouissance of the female partner, and even the fact that the woman's jouissance is crushed, to take up a term borrowed from the phenomenology of breast and nursling, in phallic nostalgia, implies that the woman is thenceforth required, and I would almost say condemned, to love the male Other only at a point situated beyond what blocks her too as desire, and which is the phallus.[12]

This comment shows how feminine jouissance is predicated, just as it is for the man, on the limit point of pleasure, although in a very different way, pointing to something beyond the phallus. Within this framework, there are many possible ways for her to orientate herself.

When a woman simply makes herself the metaphor or the symbol of the jouissance of the man, she adopts the position assigned to her by the phallic function, by subjectively identifying with the phallic object. In this case, she sacrifices her own jouissance, and has no relation other than to the man's jouissance and to his castration. Just as the law dictates, she renounces knotting her own jouissance to that of the other, and annuls the absence of that articulation. The sexual act does not satisfy her, but it does satisfy her desire to be the symbol of the desire of the Other, and for a very long time this was the only recognised mode of feminine satisfaction. In this case, the relation brought into play is that stipulated by the law; it is not sexual, but sexuated, and the man encounters nothing but his bodily complement, since she makes herself the phallic object that completes him. The orientation of the sexual relation according to the desire of the man constitutes a very common subjective position, even though the law no longer demands it. It is often found within the framework of a neurotic psychical organisation.

If, on the contrary, instead of accepting the solution offered by the sexual law, the woman refuses it, she may take up the gauntlet and try to outdo the man, decking herself out with an imaginary phallus, according to the modality of having rather than being. In our own century, the recognition of a phallic jouissance in women, including in the sexual relation, if that is what they want, has broadly favoured this position, since it allows women to be content with it. In this case, the woman devotes herself to a phallic jouissance in which she confronts the same castration as that of the man, only in different terms. She places herself entirely within the framework of the phallic function, simply by turning it upside-down. Penis envy has its place here, taking the lack of jouissance for a lack of the organ. Even though the phallic jouissance adopted by the girl when faced with the desire of the mother plays a part in this, the choice of reverting to it in a masculine way comes later. If the phallus does not give her jouissance, or if she refuses to let it do so, she decks herself out with it in order to do as well as or better than the man.

This certainly involves the renunciation of an actual sexual relation, since the jouissance in the relation to the partner is autoerotic, and it is a mirror image of the schema of the sexual law. It projects the castration imputed to her onto the man, and it achieves the same result. Nowadays this type of inversion is frequently to be found in Western societies, where it is not unusual for women to have modes of sexuality that participate only in phallic jouissance, and this may or may not be transitory. In their turn, they have laid claim to a separation between love and sex, and they approach men as objects of desire and not as desire. This mirroring of the traditional schematic position of the man can be clearly distinguished from an emergence of feminine jouissance in discourse. It consists in nothing more than extending the massive restitution of phallic jouissance to women, right into the framework of the sexual relation, in their function as subjects, and this is what characterises the development of contemporary societies. And furthermore, it substitutes this mode of jouissance for the jouissance that is specifically feminine, rather than adding itself to it in a way that would create two distinct poles.[13]

In the past, phallic jouissance was considered to be only masculine, whereas because it is jouissance of the subject, it is by nature no more masculine than feminine. It corresponds to what Freud ultimately described as a single asexual libido. Nowadays, through finding self-realisation as subjects in their personal and professional lives, many women experience themselves as being masculine or prey to psychical bisexuality, while in other ways they maintain a completely feminine position in their sexuality. And a certain type of psychoanalysis contributed to giving them this impression. The term 'bisexuality', which Freud used as a first approximation, implies that two sexes are present in one person, introducing a notion of symmetry which in fact does not exist. The idea that there could be a bit of feminine and a bit of masculine in a single subject is too vague, and does not take full account of what is at stake. The masculine is defined by there being only phallic jouissance involved, whereas in the case of the feminine, it is present in infancy, and a feminine jouissance is added later on. This does not imply that one is first masculine and then becomes feminine, because there is no specific threshold and it does not delimit two symmetrical and inverse fields. The masculine is defined by the phallic function alone, but the feminine is not entirely defined by this.

A man may feel 'feminised' by the other jouissance of a woman, confusing it with the maternal Other jouissance which he gave up in order to become a subject of speech, and which therefore cannot return without provoking anxiety. But it is possible to go beyond this confusion.

It seems, then, that there is a huge range of ways in which phallic jouissance and the jouissance of the objects of the drives can be present in both sexes, since it is they that support the subject. And added to these is another jouissance from the feminine side, in the love relation, and some men may choose to include some of this as well. More than ever, psychical sexuation is a matter of individual choice, because the law no longer constitutes anything more than one reference among many.

Specific feminine desire is initially addressed to the man's desire, because a woman's fundamental mode of access to the sexual relation remains via the desire to be desired, and it constitutes the pathway of access to her own jouissance. Freud emphasised that the woman's approach consisted in wanting to be loved rather than in loving. The position of being remains a privileged pathway to feminine jouissance, even though the desire of a man is less omnipresent than it used to be in a woman's destiny. The whole dimension of being in jouissance, which aims primarily at being desired, was misrecognised in psychoanalysis for a very long time, because the desire for being only appeared in gaps in discourse, even though it depends on it just as much as does the register of having.

Where a specifically feminine jouissance is at work in a sexual couple, it is through its articulation with the other's jouissance. This supposes that the failure of the phallic function has been identified, and the failure traced back to its exact cause, so that another solution has taken over to supplement it. Feminine logic accepts phallic logic, and recognises its limit, and then proposes a supplementary solution that constitutes its own jouissance. The lack of jouissance of the sexual couple, the mode of castration for both parties, is recognised, and something else is worked out. Taking its support from the object of desire that the phallic function makes of her, the woman lends herself to it by creating that object according to her own desire. She does not identify with this value of jouissance, but she freely invents the form that it takes. This means that to the extent that she repeats it, she creates something that supplements the jouissance that has been subtracted. From then on, there are two desires at stake, and not just one, and between them is the object to which she lends herself. Thus, feminine jouissance consists in giving this object that she does not have, obtaining jouissance from its very creation, because it compensates for the man's phallic subtraction. The object restores jouissance to her, and potency to him.

This logic constitutes a refusal of the failure of the phallus to articulate the two jouissances, and offers a supplement to it; it refuses the renunciation of jouissance involved in the phallic function, and goes beyond it. It is a refusal that does not consist in rejecting this function of the law, but rather proposes something else, something extra. It brings into being a desire and a jouissance of the woman in the interstices of discourse, which contradicts it less at the level of what is said than in the very process of saying. Feminine jouissance includes the dimension of an act, which does not consist merely in applying or repressing the position imposed – or rather, nowadays, only proposed – by the sexual law according to the unconscious myth of the Father. It brings something extra to the table, once the fault in the relation established by the law has been identified, to create an authentic 'sexual relation'. It can justifiably be called sexual because it involves two sexes with their jouissances, and not one sex with its object.[14] It adds a desire and a jouissance to the phallic function of the subject completed by their object, thus satisfying and subverting at the same time. Here we find an inversion of the terms of the law of discourse, without, however, standing in opposition to it, since it is situated in the half-spoken (*mi-dire*).

Certainly the evolution of contemporary Western societies is allowing this modality of relation to become more widespread, since in general it is taken for granted that the woman's jouissance does not consist only in being a man's woman, even if there is some jouissance involved in that. We know that something else is at stake here when she plays her part in making herself into this object, and deploys her jouissance within that framework, as a supplement to the phallic function which does not include it. Freud emphasised the narcissistic dimension of feminine love, and it deploys itself passively, through wanting to be loved, but also actively, in the sense that she comes to love in herself what she offers to the other to love. In this three-way relation she thus introduces the only element that can oppose the autoeroticism of phallic jouissance.

The woman's jouissance often involves bodily jouissance, but it does not superimpose itself on the latter, nor is it determined by it. Having jouissance of the phallus by receiving it – as the organ and as the signifier – may easily translate into orgasm, but will not necessarily do so. A woman's orgasm may occur just as frequently, or even more so, within the framework of phallic, autoerotic jouissance, whether she is alone or with a partner. The deployment of the woman's supplementary jouissance may alternate with her phallic jouissance, but it excludes her identifying with the phallus or the object, because if she did so there would be no way she could have jouissance of it.

So this feminine jouissance, too, is oriented according to the phallic subtraction that regulates and limits the sexual act, and supplements it in the imaginary register, with effects that are very real. She knows that the desire of the man is necessary to her in order for her to gain access to her own jouissance, and that the phallus fails to conjoin their jouissances. She knows that the phallic function masks the existence of this gap, and so she tries to embellish it without annulling it. By loving the Other in the man beyond the phallus, she aims at something beyond it, creating what is lacking in the imaginary register, not in a phantasy but in an act. She does not possess what she gives in this act, but she becomes it, and this gift has the effect of restoring the phallic symbol of jouissance to the man. This step-by-step construction of the sexual couple constitutes the cause of feminine jouissance.

The logic that establishes this jouissance cannot be inscribed in a law based solely on the phallic function, since it is not derived from it. The law of discourse recognises only the subject and the object, along with the signifiers to which they refer. The law is binary, while supplementary jouissance is ternary; two jouissances are knotted together by an object that stands as a third party, the object she makes of herself. This logic is not signified in discourse but forms an utterance outside it. It objects to the notion of the phallic function being all there is, but complies with it to some extent. It articulates itself with the man's phallic jouissance, and the relation formed in this way is constructed by overcoming the absence of articulation of the two of sex in the law of discourse.

When a man adopts this mode of relating, within the framework of love, he gives up on the failed phallic function, but the woman's jouissance confers on him the phallus as symbol, and he finds it again beyond the phallic function. What he loses in terms of a signifier he refinds in the form of a symbol; what he initially loses in the order of narcissism, he recuperates in what gives him jouissance. On the scale of desire, what he initially loses is recuperated on the inverted scale of jouissance. In this case, his new-found phallic jouissance can be deployed not by substituting it for the woman's other jouissance, but by articulating the two. This phallic symbol brings the woman jouissance, instead of restraining her and having her at its disposal, as the signifier does.

So the 'sexual relation' of a man and a woman can exist, and it certainly does exist in the one-ness (*l'unaire*) of a sexual couple that forms it. It is a singular knotting, worked out by and for the couple, and it could not be inscribed in discourse, which only works on behalf of one party, and would not have the capacity to act in a 'jurisprudential' way. But on the other hand, it shows that the pathway exists, and that such arrangements are possible.

At the beginning of the last century, Freud established that there was an insistence on clitoral, i.e. phallic, jouissance being repressed in the young girl, in order for vaginal jouissance to be substituted for it, and that this was a major source of neurosis. Half a century later, the Lacanian conception of the sexual relation approached it somewhat differently. The supplementary jouissance of a woman is not a substitute for anything; it is an addition, something extra, as the name implies. What is more, it allows the woman subjectively to have phallic jouissance, in her professional relations, and in motherhood, as well as in the form of clitoral sexual jouissance. But if phallic jouissance overtakes this supplementary jouissance, then it is no longer a case of a feminine jouissance, even in the name of 'women's liberation'. What is truly involved is an avoidance, whether transitory or lasting, of the complex logic that leads to femininity. However, it is also true that there cannot possibly be a universal definition of femininity.

In the same way as there are two modalities of sexuation leading to failure of the sexual relation, there are also two fundamental ways of dealing with the gap in the 'sexual relation' that is determined by the phallic function. The first, the masculine one, increases the scope of the phallic function and its major signifier, both of which annul the gap; the other, the feminine one, compensates for it by partially renouncing the phallic function. Partially within discourse, and partially outside it, femininity is constructed within the framework of a particular encounter, even if it is with God, as was the case with the mystics. To a man, femininity reveals just what a gap, what an absence of conjunction there is in sexual jouissance, whereas as long as the feminine object he thinks he has jouissance of continues to appear to him as his complement, femininity is annulled and repressed. The gap there is only revealed through the solution to it that is proposed by a woman.

In a love relation, when a man takes the step of renouncing the failed phallic function in order to adopt the other jouissance, he does not obliterate the gap but rather participates in adding something extra to it. The way this works is simple in the sense that there is, if one can put it this way, room for two within supplementary jouissance and its logic, whereas in the jouissance and the logic of the phallic function, there is room only for one and his 'other half'. This is how the sexual couple is inscribed in discourse according to the law, whereas it is united in the real when supplementary jouissance is involved. There is thus the possible process of a real union between a man and a woman, in spite of the structure of the law and the non-relation it engenders in a universal sense. It explains, on the fringes of the law and in the silence of the space outside discourse, how couples have always formed between a man and a woman, randomly within or without marriage or partnership, and always through 'elective affinities'; and out of their encounter they have created a locus for working out a supplement to the law's disinterest in love, and have thus made the lack less oppressive.

VII. The absence of relation between two sexes in discourse

So we have seen that it is possible to create a relation between two in the sexual couple, even though it is complex and slow to work out, and even though it has proved to be fragile in terms of marriage/partnership. But it does not exist within a discourse, and is only partially supported by it. The grammar of the sexual law, formed through the interpretation of the sexual relation in terms of phallic jouissance, never allowed the articulation of the jouissances of the two sexes. The biological disjunction of the modes of jouissance of the two sexes is only made more extreme through the discourse of the sexual law. If their relation may be inscribed there, it is not sexual, involving only phallic jouissance and its object. In this sense it is '*hommosexual*' because it depends only on the substance of the man (*l'homme*), who because of this is 'swindled, because all he encounters is his bodily complement'.[15] Or the relation that is established knots together phallic jouissance and the other jouissance, and in this case it is certainly sexual, but is not inscribed in discourse, because it is beyond the phallic function that governs it. So an impossibility becomes apparent: that of inscribing an actual sexual relation in discourse, in the sense of one that knots two sexes together.

In the current state of discourse, such an impossibility seems at first sight to be the consequence of the paternal Oedipal system of our symbolic institutions that the unconscious generates, and which in our time has undergone a major modification. Conceived of as a 'complementary' relationship for the man, who possesses a phallus both regulated and taken away by the Father – with the woman who is the phallus as partial object, as the child is for the mother – he can avoid the evocation of incest with the mother through his confrontation with the desire of the woman. This law seems to be derived from the prohibition of incest, as a radical way of assuring that it is respected.

Even though nowadays it no longer has the force of law, the non-relation of the sexes still persists, and is indeed more and more visible. Since the law is no longer imposed, and marriage no longer masks the absence of a relation, the latter has become more obvious. The point is that even if the sexual act might re-integrate a few subjective attributes that were elided by the law, it does not amount to making a relation of two between the sexes. In this relation, an obstacle has been recognised since the dawn of time, widely debated and discussed in a number of ancient civilisations, and which persists and seems to be impossible to eliminate. In the Western world, contemporary sexuality has been liberated, and in the Eastern world has developed, too, in spite of the upsurge of radical movements which aim to combat this 'liberation'. The way sexual practices and symptoms have developed is clear, but the human 'sexual relation', both in terms of the sexual act and the relation between the sexes, still involves a gap.

Our symbolic institutions themselves have delineated this absence of duality in their discourses. Our signifying system has borrowed from the modality of phallic jouissance to create the grammar of a discourse based on the phallic One, the relation of 'one plus object *a*' in the law. The Father of the Oedipus complex appropriated this by having the phallus at his unique disposal, in the name of the prohibition of incest, depriving the mother and the child of it. The same terms converged to determine sexuation and the sexual relation.

So the sexual law has two sources, one of which is superimposed on the other. It is first of all a grammar that draws into discourse the particularity of penile jouissance, and through the cut that this involves deduces a supposedly complementary sexuated relation. But this law is also what is created by the mythical Father, when he is added to this as a transcendent agent, spanning both the Oedipus complex and the sexual relation. As the belief in the Father diminished, or even collapsed altogether, the sexual law began to loosen its grip. And from then on, the absence of a relation of two sexes in discourse has been quite obvious.

This impossibility has shown itself to be much greater than we might have thought. The development of the social bond has allowed the establishment of a more dignified relation between the sexes, but in discourse it is still not inscribed as a relation between two parties. It continues to work itself out in individual cases without becoming law, without having a universal application, through speech put into action in each sexual couple, rather than as a dictum of discourse. Just because the law constructed according to an autoerotic logic has loosened its grip, it does not mean that the two of sex can knot itself together in discourse. Just because a woman's phallic jouissance has added itself to that of the man, whether through orgasm or otherwise, it does not form a real sexual relation, because where there is equivalence there can be no relation. When this relation does exist, it can only be singular, unary, and it cannot be inscribed.

So the question raised by the 'sexual relation' is infinitely greater than that of the influence of discourse on sex as such, because it concerns the whole gamut of our symbolic institutions. We now need to explore the whole range of these institutions and the way they operate both on and from the sexual relation. For so long, the logic of the phallic function has held sway over all this, constructing its signifiers and determining what is said and what is not said, while masking the absence of the dual relation in the very structures it creates. Now that it is no longer the unique agency organising sex and subjectivity, the veil has been lifted.

Notes

1 Lacan, *Anxiety*, op. cit., p. 269.
2 Lacan considered the former expression to be inadequate with regard to what is at stake, because one ought to say 'premature detumescence', since that is what matters. However, it is frequently said that an orgasm without ejaculation may not involve detumescence, and this had already been observed in the sexual traditions of ancient China. For this reason, 'premature ejaculation' is not that far off the mark.
3 Lacan put it like this: 'The value of forbidden jouissance at the precise point, at the point of the organ constituted by the phallus, is carried over as object libido. Contrary to what people say, that it is narcissistic libido that is the reservoir from which object libido will have to extract itself'. Jacques Lacan, *Logic of the Phantasy*, seminar of 19 April 1967.
4 Here is the complete sentence: 'The only insertion point necessary for any sexual ideology, this subtraction of jouissance somewhere, that's the essence of it'. Jacques Lacan, *Logic of the Phantasy*, seminar of 12 April 1967.
5 Here, for example, is another formulation: 'It's from this suspense of the male organ that a function takes on its value, in relation to this hole, this gap of the castration complex, in an inverted way'. Jacques Lacan, *Logic of the Phantasy*, seminar of 24 May 1967.
6 For example, in Lacan, *Encore*, op. cit., pp. 80–1.

7 'What he's looking for is minus phi, what she is lacking – but that is male stuff. She knows very well, let me tell you, that she is not missing anything. Or rather that the way in which lack operates in female development is not linked to the level where it is aimed at by male desire, when it is a question for him of a sadistic search that I emphasised this year, which aims to make the supposed place of lack in the partner appear. That is what has to be mourned'. Lacan, *Anxiety*, op cit., p. 199, translation modified. And he adds: 'Everyone drones on about *penisneid*. It's here that we have to emphasise the difference'.

8 Lacan developed the idea of this displacement in his seminar of 19 April 1967, *The Logic of Phantasy*, op. cit.

9 The philosopher Jean-Luc Marion, in *Le phénomène érotique*, Grasset, 2003, put forward an interesting conception of the flesh of each individual being eroticised by the desire of the other, which works like a chiasma in a mirror. This remains true within the framework of desire, but the dimension of jouissance itself is dissymmetrical; one of the two jouissances remains adrift, and the chiasma does not occur.

10 Lacan, *The Other Side of Psychoanalysis*, *The Seminar of Jacques Lacan, Book 17*, New York, Norton, 2007, p. 73, translation modified.

11 He continued thus: 'In truth, I'm sure of it, it's from this first basic recognition that the necessity of a medium is born, the intermediary of the screen constituted by the phantasy, that is, that infinite complexity, that richness of desire with all its appetites, all its spaces, the whole map it creates, all its effects at the level of the slopes we call neurotic, psychotic or perverse, and which are inserted precisely in that eternal gap between the two jouissances'. Jacques Lacan, *The Psychoanalytic Act*, seminar of 21 February 1968. We can see the difficulty here in trying to express the function of this object, which both responds to this disjunction through the phantasy, while at the same time blocking and intensifying it.

12 Lacan, *Anxiety*, op. cit., p. 304, translation modified.

13 According to some publications, the development of contemporary American society includes a large number of couples formed in this way. For example, in Sonya Rhodes and Susan Schneider's *The Alpha Woman Meets Her Match*, New York, HarperCollins, 2014, the denomination of alpha and beta sums up the positions we can describe in our own field in terms of having or being the phallus respectively. Others aim to invert the terms of the old sexual law towards the side of women, in a mirroring process; see, for example, Hanna Rosin, *The End of Men: And the Rise of Women*, New York, Riverhead, 2012. Rosin writes that: 'In 2012, sexual relations with no tomorrow sum up the essence of femininity: liberty, independence, autonomy'. This sentence, one among many examples, shows how far such an inversion is from what was elaborated in the Freudian/Lacanian field about femininity, where the restitution of phallic jouissance to women, both essential and historic, was not enough to bring about an orientation towards a specific feminine jouissance, which is of another order.

14 The term 'sexual' is used here in the sense of involving two sexes, but obviously in the strictest sense it also concerns partners of the same sex. We should also note that the type of relation constructed on the basis of the supplementary jouissance of a woman is sometimes described in a lesbian relation.

15 Jacques Lacan, *Logic of the Phantasy*, seminar of 31 May 1967.

Chapter 4

The veiling of non-conjunction

One might well wonder how something so vast, so central and so fundamental to the human condition as the absence of any articulation of the relation between the two sexes has managed to remain veiled. When the so-called complementary relation that appeared in the law as if it were a relation between two was shown to be anything but that, and when the metaphor of Genesis ceased to be the object of universal belief that had given it the force of law, it was clear that a real relation between two sexes was something quite different. But it also became clear that the latter did not figure in any discourse, and could only exist – when it did exist – in particular cases, in silence, outside of discourse. In order for this to occur, it required a fundamental reworking of social bonds, and a significant reduction in the role of the factors that contributed to masking the initial absence.

There were indeed a number of factors that contributed to the covering-up of the gap in the articulation between the two sexes. The difficulty in the relation between the sexes can be observed at two connected levels: the discourse of the law, and the disjunction between the modes of jouissance of the two sexes. We need to isolate the different factors that have drawn a veil over this fact, so that we can understand the reality that we are dealing with.

I. The veil of prohibition

There is no doubt that prohibition is the most effective way of veiling the sexual non-relation as well as the disjunction between the sexes. For so long, the prohibition of any sexual jouissance that fell outside the framework of the law, and its application in the various laws regarding marriage, masked the fact that the law decreed that only one sex was entitled to subjectivity, and elided that of the other. The prohibition covered up the fact that in the institutions of language, there was no question of there being two involved in sex, but only of the one and his object. Once this relation was presented as a relation of two sexes, with the woman as object appearing to complement the man, and a woman was deemed to amount to nothing more than that, then the lack of there being two in the relation was no longer apparent. The entire symbolic order proceeded on this basis, because all the functions it included – that of the Father, which was its cornerstone, that of

DOI: 10.4324/9781003285984-5

the phallus, which was at his command, and the sexuation derived from it – all depended on the same articulation where a single signifier of desire and jouissance was present for both sexes.

What is more, when jouissance is prohibited, the question disappears about what it actually consists of, and the disjunction of the jouissances of the partners in the sexual act fades into the background. The prohibition of sexual jouissance, vested in the mythical Father of the law and religion, is centred on the founding law of humanity, that of the prohibition of incest, but it went far beyond it. Any object that had a trait of the incestuous object would be feared and rejected as incestuous, even if in reality this was not at all the case. The incestuous imaginings that appear in phantasies, in our time as much as in the past, and perhaps even more so, would be taken literally as if they really involved incest, and as such would require punishment.

The symbolic agent of this is the Father introduced by Freud in the myth of the primal Father, who himself had jouissance without limits while prohibiting everyone else from having any. Subsequently killed by his rebellious sons, he was restored to his full rights and powers through the invention of the God of monotheism; and he remains a major construction of the unconscious. No matter that such an original Father could not possibly have existed and been killed in every human horde; his function is still patently at work in the unconscious and in the institutions of language. The most fundamental modalities of Fathers in humanity operate along the same lines. Everywhere, in various forms, the rule was imposed symbolically on all the others by one who was exempt from it; everywhere, the agent of castration was the one who did not submit to it, and jouissance was forbidden by the one who had no limit to his own.

With recent developments regarding this agency of the Father, with the loss of belief in him, the prohibition has gone up in smoke, and what it covered up has now been exposed. The disjunction of jouissances has been revealed, and at the same time a logic other than that of the all-phallic has come to light. The phallic function is clearly opposed to the conjunction of two jouissances, both in the sexual act and in discourse. In the order of language, the absence of the sexual 'two' has been revealed. The jouissance of women has entered, in a general sense, into discourse; as ever, women's specific jouissance operates in the silence outside discourse, while it is clear that their phallic jouissance is inscribed in discourse without being articulated with that of men.

So the absence of the inscription of the 'sexual relation' begins to appear as an impossibility that was concealed by prohibition, rather than as being the actual result of the prohibition of sexual jouissance. This impossibility persists in a historical context in which our symbolic order is still broadly constructed according to structures that involve the function of the Father, the Name of the Father, religious, social and patriarchal. It still largely ties together the different registers of our subjectivity, those of the body, of jouissance, and of the law which, however, as things stand, does not yet fully allow other modes of articulation. And yet other modes of knotting together are emerging in our structures; some are in the process of being worked out, and new and varied modalities of the 'names of the Father' are already functioning. Even though it may occur in a different way, the latter are also generating the necessary knotting between the different subjective registers.

The phallus, around which desire, the law and sexuality are organised, now functions rather differently, and less as the mediator of desires and jouissances between the sexes. It has become clear that each sex has a relation to it, without that creating in itself a relation between them. Formed as a concept by the unconscious to resolve the problem of a gap in the conjunction of the sexes, and imposed as a law by the majority of civilisations, as a unique signifier it cuts through this conjunction and reinforces it. At the point where there is a problem concerning the two, it retains only one, to the extent that it refocuses on, and even makes absolute, the lack of articulation between them, and stands in opposition to a relation between the two. Invented as a signifier to eradicate the gap between the two jouissances, by symbolising only one of them, it can be used for anything except at the exact point where it has been created. It cannot serve to articulate the jouissance of man with that of woman, since, in order to resolve the non-conjunction of their jouissances, it was forged on the premise that one jouissance had to be set aside. It has become clear that the phallic function, which the law bases on a division of the 'sexual relation', cannot serve as the foundation for the relation of two, since it no longer articulates it. That is why, while the joys of phallic jouissance cannot be denied, and while the new woman of this century does not belittle the pleasure she has in enjoying it in every possible domain, it still does not compensate for the failure of the 'relation' that has been revealed in our time. Until then, the failure had stemmed from the fact that the phallic function was operative only on the side of the man, but when it operates only on the side of the woman, it leads in a symmetrical way to precisely the same failure.

In both discourse and the sexual act, the phallus presents itself as the commanding signifier that subtracts and limits jouissance, rather than as the one that articulates one jouissance with another. Femininity objects to this, at least in part, as does neurosis, only in a less effective fashion. Homosexuality objects to it by refusing the relation between two sexes, and takes the gamble that a sexual relation within the same sex will avoid the hindrance of access to the other. The disappearance of the prohibition of sexual jouissance has restored the prohibition of incest to its rightful place in the real, and means that incestuous imaginings are no longer subject to punishment. Nowadays, access to sex is no longer limited by the prohibitions of discourse, apart from whatever is inflicted by the unconscious; but it still comes up against the impasses of sexual jouissance.

II. Negating the subtraction of jouissance

In the sexual act itself, many factors contribute to enabling the disjunction not to appear, and to annulling the fact that a subtraction of jouissance tends to be substituted for a conjunction of the two. The factors that mask this absence of two in the sexual act are very powerful, and the effects of discourse play a significant part.

'Having jouissance of' rather than 'making [them] have jouissance' allows the lack of conjunction of jouissances to be annulled, and it may remain completely veiled. Other than in symptomatic cases, the subtraction of jouissance may not appear at all.

We might think that the nature of satisfaction in the sexual act is a question that we don't need to ask, since it has always been considered – even by Freud – as the most intense satisfaction there is, even if not the greatest. However, it is more complex than it might appear. In a general way, the cessation of jouissance through the male orgasm followed by detumescence, unless it is a symptom, is not considered to be a subtraction but a satisfying limit. And, as Lacan pointed out, since detumescence in reality represents the fact that there is jouissance beyond it,[1] that jouissance as such lies beyond this limit that subtracts it. It is therefore the subtraction of jouissance that gives satisfaction. In this act, one is not satisfied by what one might think.

In psychoanalytic conceptualisation, satisfaction and jouissance are two very different things. Satisfaction is on the side of the function of the subject, regulated by the homoeostasis of the pleasure principle, which insists that there should not be too much jouissance, because beyond that limit one is in the realm of anxiety, or even of suffering. So the aim of satisfaction is not the same as the aim of jouissance, even if they partially overlap. The threshold of the pleasure principle is eminently variable from subject to subject, since for each individual it depends on their relation to jouissance, to the law and to the Other beyond the partner.

Jouissance, which in the psychoanalytic sense is distinct from orgasm, and may or may not include it, constitutes a psychical economy organised by language and the drives beyond the limit of pleasure. In its essence it is that which goes beyond the satisfaction of the subject, who remains this side of jouissance while nonetheless aiming at it. Lacan used a deliberately equivocal sentence to define the function of male orgasm in the sexual act: '*L'orgasme emporte la satisfaction*'.[2] This means both that it satisfies and, with the ambiguity of '*emporter*', which means both 'brings' and 'takes away', that it removes satisfaction. This polarity is central to what is involved in the sexual act. This ambiguous relation to satisfaction comes from the fact that it is closely bound up with anxiety. Obeying the limit of the pleasure principle, interrupting jouissance at the point where it could provoke anxiety, orgasm seems in some way to surf on anxiety, occurring when anxiety arises, in order to put an end to it.

'*La petite mort*' ('the little death'), as male orgasm is known in French, may constitute this anticipation of an anxiety along the pathway of the call to jouissance, by putting the organ out of action following ejaculation. The anticipation of feminine jouissance provokes anxiety in both the man and the woman, but if it occurs, it can have the same result. For the man, it is a sign of his phallic potency, but it may have the paradoxical effect of his seeing himself as an instrument of satisfaction. The male orgasm shuts down the anxiety of the approach of the female orgasm at the same time as it takes away satisfaction. That is why, as Lacan emphasised, it is the only form of anxiety that ends well. And that is where satisfaction begins, for the sexual couple as an entity: in trying to come out of it well.

The satisfaction of a subject formed in the unconscious through separating from jouissance, reproduces itself in a similar way and keeps its distance from jouissance wherever the subject is involved. The subject is compliant with the law of the pleasure principle that forbids this jouissance, so that the phallic subtraction that puts an end to sexual jouissance gives satisfaction, and is not experienced as a subtraction. Even though this limit, made flesh through detumescence, signals another jouissance beyond it, it is annulled to an even greater extent if the act brings satisfaction, whereas if the act does not bring satisfaction, the limit appears starkly. The sexual act shows the action of a signifier on the real, as in every act, but jouissance is both summoned to it and subtracted from in more than with other acts.

It is hard to conceive of a limit that brings satisfaction while also subtracting jouissance. Detumescence appears to be a sort of natural law that punctuates the act, and the male orgasm cannot be repeated straight away, which accentuates its biological distance from the woman's, which is slow to occur and calls for a repetition afterwards, leading to well-known subjective consequences. Its triggering occurs according to a subjective decision of the unconscious, which gives it the air of 'the vocative of a commandment',[3] which is how Lacan put it, which can easily lead to the idea of a divine agency commanding it.

It is indeed the unconscious that gives the command, according to the subject's relation to their own jouissance and to that of the other, but this unconscious command acts upon a physiology that has its own characteristics. It seems obvious that the subtraction of jouissance is all the greater when detumescence occurs prematurely, and it can certainly have the air of being an escape, an objection to both one's own jouissance and that of the other. It is lessened when the interruption occurs later, and leaves more room for jouissance, but anorgasmia in men represents just as significant an objection. Anorgasmia in women has the same characteristic of subtracting jouissance, too, but of course does not have the same effects. So if the limit of the relation is satisfying, we can imagine that it would not appear as a subtraction, although the latter is structurally present and contributes to fabricating the fundamental signifier of the speaking being, that of the phallic function, with its logic. This punctuation of the sexual act by masculine jouissance creates the organising signifier, while feminine jouissance is not obliged to stop, and the possible absence of orgasm does not stand in the way of reproduction at all here.

In fact, this non-conjunction is the result of both modes of jouissance, rather than of just one, since the high threshold for the woman's attainment of orgasm is compounded by the low threshold for the man's. The limit point of detumescence has all the more impact when the woman's orgasmic threshold is higher, when her orgasm occurs later, and this threshold is also just as subjectively influenced, even though in part it obeys certain physiological constants. Conversely, this limit is experienced far less when the woman's orgasmic threshold is lower and she attains orgasm more frequently.

The woman may be just as satisfied by the limit imposed by her partner's subjectivity. It may be that his unconscious position forbids him to abandon himself to the jouissance coming from the Other, or there may be an element of deliberate renunciation; either way, the satisfaction is marked by the same type of regulation by the pleasure principle as that which governs detumescence: not too much jouissance, whether it involves orgasm or not. In order for the pathway towards jouissance to be found and followed, it is necessary that the subject does not intervene.

But of course, the woman's subjective lack of satisfaction is present in cases where the limit of the sexual act is tangible due to premature detumescence. This is only exacerbated by a discourse that turns the female orgasm into a demand, which weighs on the woman just as much as on the man, affecting the sexual couple's jouissance. Even when satisfaction is present, for some men as well as some women a sense of failure, and even reactions of rejection and depression, may appear when the orgasm is not produced. Because nowadays satisfaction masks the fact to a lesser extent than in the past that it is indeed a subtraction that puts an end to the sexual act, rather than a conjunction of jouissances. As modern knowledge of sex develops, sexological advice is being given which is implicitly or explicitly aimed at the difficulty of bringing together the two modes of orgasm, bearing in mind the rapidity of one and the slowness of the other.

This difficulty of sexual conjunction was unveiled in the last century, when prohibitions faded and sexual couples no longer stayed together for life, as the law had once dictated. Trying to achieve conjunction has become a gamble. Just as the rites of Ancient China recommended that men should avoid detumescence by delaying ejaculation, and Medieval India offered advice on how to satisfy the sexual partner, modern manuals of sexology spell our various methods with the same aims, but of course without any ritual or sacred function.

But there is no technique showing how to knot together a relation between two parties, or how two psychical jouissances can be articulated, while making space for love in the sexual couple. And no technique could possibly do so, since that mode of relation is not inscribed anywhere and cannot be universalised. It is always a case of a unique invention, in the form of a new construction resulting in a relation between two unconsciouses, and it cannot be generalised even if a logic can be defined by it.[4] Psychoanalysis has contributed to enabling this process, because it tends to bring about the fall of the functions that stand in its way – the phallus, the object a – and to allow a crossing of the all-phallic logic of the Oedipus complex and of neurosis, allowing for the emergence of something different

III. Detumescence as symbol of satisfaction

There is another factor that contributes to masking the fact that the sexual act is punctuated by a subtraction rather than a conjunction of the jouissances of the two sexes. Lacan pointed out that the detumescent organ presents itself as the symbol of a satisfaction with nothing left over;[5] it is the image of the act having been accomplished, and that there is nothing more to expect. And to be sure, very often nothing more is expected. But that is an illusion, because detumescence masks a limit, while at the same time being that which produces it. Subjective satisfaction is thus, in a sense, deceived as the very thing that subtracts jouissance presents the subtraction as a satisfying conclusion. And therefore, the way the act unfolds as a whole is oriented according to this modality of its conclusion.

The detumescent penis may indeed be the symbol of a satisfaction without a remainder when it is precisely the thing that puts a stop to jouissance, because it bears witness to the fact that the limit has been reached. If the penis remained erect following orgasm, which can sometimes happen, the expectation of jouissance would continue, and a beyond to this pleasure would still be very present, and as a result it would not appear to be without remainder. A remainder of jouissance would be aimed at, a desire would persist. In order for this limit imposed by the pleasure principle to be effective, it is necessary for pleasure to have occurred, and that it cannot be repeated immediately. And even if it is pursued beyond this limit, it is still in reference to it.

Lacan emphasised that the anxiety around the limit of the sexual act and the call to jouissance of the other can be resolved if one allows oneself to be subjected to it. The limit does indeed bring satisfaction, and to a considerable extent: 'satisfaction' is even the word that occurs in polls about sexual satisfaction. The limit can be pushed beyond pleasure only where there is a will to jouissance, which is no longer in the register of pleasure, or, therefore, of satisfaction. Orgasm accompanied by detumescence incarnates the limit between pleasure and jouissance, satisfying the former while masking the fact that it subtracts the latter. This model of sexual satisfaction in terms of stimulation, discharge and withdrawal of functionality, is so entrenched that it provides the model for all schemas of satisfaction of the drive, but there is no other drive that includes the materialisation of the limit that provides a separation from the jouissance beyond it. The schema of the discharge of the drive, entailing a limit imposed by the pleasure principle, and described very early on by Freud, clearly borrows from this, even though he does not mention it. Because ejaculation is followed by detumescence, the male orgasm has the unique characteristic of delimiting a drive with a high point of pleasure followed by its termination. This is the reason why it has been borrowed to create a logic.

The jouissance of sex is the only one to include a bodily cessation that goes in tandem with satisfaction, and in which the subtraction of the jouissance that might occur beyond this point does not appear, except in symptomatic cases. Lacan pointed out that instead of a minus, a zero appears, and the subtraction is annulled.[6] And at the same time, so is the jouissance that has not taken place. The negated subtraction produces subjective satisfaction, with detumescence as its symbol, constituted as a zero moment when in fact it is a minus, yet a minus that is veiled. On that basis the objects that cause desire are constructed, masking the fact that the desire linked to them is caused by a loss of jouissance. So something has to annul this lack of jouissance, the negativity inscribed at the heart of the sexual relation, which causes the investment of an object to appear in the imagination as starting from zero.

In the discourse of the law, subjectivity is more of a male issue, since the cut that correlates with the orgasm concerns him more closely. But the subjective function of the woman has its roots in the same satisfaction, which also negates the subtraction and the absence of the two as a conjunction of jouissances. Because the characteristic of a subject of the unconscious, and thus of language, in a close relation with the pleasure principle that governs them, is to take the minus of jouissance as a zero, organising the causation of their desire on that basis – on the basis of a zero and not of a minus. As Lacan emphasised, not without humour: when the desire of the man stays this side of a certain jouissance of the woman, it is by its nature going to keep her serene, and even reassured, because she doesn't have to worry about his intentions. This also provides the resolution for the anxiety she too experiences along the pathway to the jouissance of the other, as well as her own. Hence, for her too, remaining this side of jouissance is a good thing from the point of view of the pleasure principle.

The masked subtraction of jouissance in the sexual act thus satisfies the entire system of the subject, since it is formed at the subject's origin, by separating from a primary jouissance as object of the maternal Other, and from then on cannot bear too much jouissance. Certainly it is difficult to isolate this masked subtraction, this replacement of a minus by a zero, since the jouissance is in some way a too-much, and so suppressing it does not make a minus but actually a zero. But the definition of a limit is that it subtracts what is beyond it, even if what is beyond it is not a good thing, and from that point it conditions the organisation of what is this side of the limit.

In the sexual act, the subject is in this sense situated on the same side as the phallus that Lacan defined as the conscientious objection made by one of the two sexes to the service it had to render to the other. Such an objection certainly culminates in premature ejaculation or impotence, which obey the pleasure principle in a radical way, occurring immediately if the call to jouissance becomes too anxiety-provoking. But as we have emphasised, there is another subjective modality of the phallus, defined as causing jouissance in a woman rather than having jouissance of her. This is a phallic mode which plays a part in constructing an actual sexual relation between a man and a woman: it does not constitute an objection to the service to be rendered to the other, but rather to the sexual law itself, just as feminine jouissance does.

IV. Satisfaction of the limit

It is not unthinkable, then, that the function of the subject may be satisfied by a limit, if each partner moves towards the point where the union of jouissances is supposed to occur, and then encounters something other than what was expected; and then finds that the expectation recedes along with a certain relief engendered by the limit. Whether the subject is a man or a woman, satisfaction comes from the failure of jouissance, as a beyond to pleasure, and is simultaneously reinforced because the failure is masked. The subject approaches jouissance while obeying the limit that demands that there shall not be too much jouissance, and is satisfied if the excess is subtracted, the more so since it is not apparent that this occurs thanks to the function that is itself the agent of subtraction.

Just like the phallus, the subject of the unconscious fades at the approach of jouissance, or sometimes may even refuse completely to have any jouissance if they make themself the symbol of the jouissance of the Other. In reality, the incitement to jouissance that is present for everyone in the way current discourses are evolving causes a considerable number of people to refuse jouissance altogether.

The structural subtraction of jouissance within the sexual couple does not actually make an appearance, other than in symptomatic cases, because the minus is replaced by a zero, on the basis of which the series of objects of desire is constituted. It seems that the man's desire, aiming at an object, comes out of nowhere, whereas in reality it is caused by the loss of jouissance that concludes the sexual relation. The subject appears to be pushed from a zero point towards the objects he aims at, whereas in reality he is pushed from a minus point.[7] We have seen how the feminine object that completes the man is formed in this way. The cut in the sexual act causes a specific form of object of phantasy, created as a value of jouissance to be refound, and its origin engenders a logic that is particular to the relation of the subject to desire. The desire that comes from phallic jouissance is caused on the basis of this mode of the cut and is then carried forward as a value of jouissance, but the cause remains masked, and the desire is perceived simply as one that aims at an object. Consequently, the lack of jouissance is annulled. For a man, having a sexual relation with a woman becomes the equivalent of having the woman, having jouissance of her, because the phallic object takes the place of a compensation for the preceding subtraction, and so it goes on. Similarly, penetrating her is known as 'having her'.

Subsequently, the subtraction causes a desire, while at the same time being negated and carried over to an object as partner, whether it is the same one or someone else. The new object takes the place of the one that has been subtracted, assuming its value in terms of jouissance, and logically takes on the signification of a phallic object, since it compensates for and fills up the space left by phallic subtraction. The formation of the object of phantasy in this way contributes to the non-appearance of either the subtraction of jouissance or the difficulty of conjoining the jouissances of the partners of the two sexes. This mode of desire is specifically the one involved in and comprised by phallic jouissance alone, it is the desire of the man when he refuses to go beyond the point of this jouissance, and in this sense it is autoerotic. But it can be the same for a woman if she also refuses to go beyond a subjective phallic jouissance, without adopting the modality of feminine jouissance.

The process of carrying forward a subtracted jouissance takes place beyond the field of the sexual act, at the very heart of discourse. It is easy to observe how a pleasure, a jouissance, or an object that is taken away from us pushes us, in the sense of a drive, towards the goal of refinding some equivalent. Any subtraction along the pathway to jouissance functions in this way to cause desire, creating that kind of value. Traditionally, the desired woman was the one who refused herself, or gave herself only by degree. Throughout the ages, *Cartes du Tendre* have been organised according to the principle of subtraction, which causes the subject's desire. Nowadays, it is no longer the subtraction of a woman from the man's desire that organises her sexuated position, unless perhaps it happens to be her subjective and singular way of doing so; things have changed for her. Besides, the subtraction of a man from the woman's desire may equally be a cause of desire for the woman when she adopts the phallic jouissance of the subject in the sexual encounter.

The satisfaction of the sexual act, therefore, has something illusory or misleading about it, since it relies on the fact that a failure of jouissance occurs and remains masked. For the man, it is the more misleading because the carrying forward of the lack constitutes his partner as a phantasy object, and he can only reach her in the form of Eve created imaginarily from his own subtracted phallic body part, as a bodily complement. This does not exclude the possibility that a man may adopt another mode of desire and of jouissance.

In a great many cases, this satisfaction is just as misleading for the woman. Either she will carry forward the jouissance that has been subtracted from her in the sexual act onto a man, whom she takes to be a phallic object; or her desire will consist in promoting herself as a phallic object, aiming to cause and maintain the man's desire, while sacrificing her own jouissance, thereby remaining within a logic that obeys the phallic function. In this case, the lack of jouissance in the sexual relation does not go unnoticed, but it is treated in a way that does not resolve it any more than the phallic logic does. There is only one case where satisfaction does not deceive, because it stems from something else, and leads to another kind of jouissance.

V. Feminine jouissance compensates for the disjunction

The mode of jouissance that is specifically feminine, where it occurs, is probably the factor that best succeeds in masking the sexual disjunction, just as it makes the absence of the two of sex less apparent in discourse. Compensating for it is indeed the best way of ensuring that it does not appear. The logic that leads to this, unlike earlier modes of response, is not based on a negation and a repression; instead, it adds something that overcomes it. Through introducing this third term of the object she makes of herself, a woman achieves the realisation of a union of jouissances, as long as the man agrees to give up the position given to him by the law, in order to realise a conjunction based on other factors. This suppleance recognises the gap that is at stake both in the sexual act and in discourse, and seeks a pathway that will enable the knotting of the jouissance of one with that of the other. It involves a refusal to acknowledge the defect in the union of jouissances, not through renouncing the union, but rather in taking it upon oneself to overcome the defect. It holds especially true here, and is demonstrable, that jouissance as such demands that there be two jouissances, and that giving up on knotting them together means giving up on jouissance. Jouissance means jouissance of the Other, not in the sense of the subjective genitive, where the Other would have jouissance of the subject, but in the sense of the objective genitive, which consists in having jouissance by making oneself the object of the Other's desire, beyond its failure to unite them.

The logic that leads to a feminine jouissance is based initially on the phallic logic of the law, which positions the subject solely on the side of the man. Within that logic, assuming the function of object that she represents for the desire of the man, she inverts the positioning and creates the object that she makes of herself in order to offer it to the man. Within this framework, something quite different occurs from the inversion that consists in also making herself a subject, and consequently the subject of a phallic jouissance; this could only lead to a position mirroring that of the man, which is a common cause of phallic discord. In order to make herself into this object, in order to lend herself to it without identifying with it, she has to imagine it, to create it in her imagination. Lacan observed that in reality it is this object that is active here, while the subject is subverted. Through this active gift of the object, in the sense of the object giving itself, the phallus – which the subtraction inherent in the sexual relation has removed – can be restored in the imaginary register.

So it is no longer the case that in the sexual relation there is the one who, as subject, believes that he has jouissance of the other, and is prevented from so doing by the subtraction inherent in the functioning of the penis; nor of the other, who makes herself the symbol of his jouissance, and for that reason cannot herself have jouissance. It is rather a case of the jouissance of she who actively makes herself the object of desire of the man, and in so doing confers the phallus on him in a way other than through the law of the Father. A woman can have jouissance in this very creation, which consists in giving what she does not have, to the one who thus comes to be provided with the phallus in a new way.

This process is complex and difficult to grasp. One might, for example, make the following objection: if this position consists in voluntarily proving the rightness of the sexual law of the phallic function, in what way can it be deemed supplementary? In reality, it is not a question of a straightforward application of the law, but rather of a division of the woman's position between her desire, which constructs the relation, and the object of desire of the other, which she makes herself into with this aim. Here we discover the functioning of a particular mode of subjectivity, which actually manages to leave aside the function of the subject while lending itself to a certain function as object for the other, but still staying on course where one's own desire is concerned.

In psychoanalysis, when this type of position began to appear in Lacan's formulations, it seemed to represent a new type of logic, and a type of functioning that had not previously been identified conceptually. It brought into play an act that was not entirely situated in a single register, based on imaginary elements while also being very real. And this new logic subverted the lines drawn in traditional logic, where there was no contradiction, setting up an object that was active and a subject as subverted, quite the opposite of what obtained in the law of the phallic function. This new logic becomes all the more important by not only approaching the real more closely, unlike that of the all-phallic, which keeps its distance from the real, but also by proving to be the same type of logic as the one at work in artistic creation, in thinking and in psychoanalytic practice. There, too, psychoanalysts lend themselves to being the object in the transference, obviously without identifying with it, and always staying on course where their desire as analyst is concerned.

This process that unfolds in the imaginary has very real effects, and allows for a knotting of two jouissances within the sexual couple, since they have this object in common. When Lacan remarked that the two of the 'sexual relation' could not achieve a direct articulation, he studied the topology of the Borromean knot, which is characterised precisely by not knotting elements two by two, but through the intermediary of a third.[8] This had enabled him to understand how feminine jouissance operates this kind of knotting, between a woman's desire and that of the other, through the intermediary of a third term, which consists in the object that she makes of herself. The woman, who is defined by the sexual law as the one who lacks, presents herself in such a relation as the one who gives what is lacking, and this inversion *which is her very jouissance* reinforces the potency of the symbol that she confers on the other. In so doing, her love comes into play, in the sense of giving what she does not have, which happens quite differently from giving what one does have. This is why for a woman, love often begins with the sexual act, while for a man, if he conceives of it as the gift of what he does have, it may well mark the end of love.

The way in which the woman's supplementary jouissance can make up for a lack in the sexual relation does not, then, consist in annulling the lack but rather in creating a supplement capable of forming a relation. The object she imagines allows her desire to participate just as much as the man's, to the extent that she has to invent it for that particular man. A woman's love emerges from her jouissance consenting to the man's desire, and more than that, it invents the object of his desire through a creation. This forms the pathway for access to her own jouissance, in a way that is quite different from merely representing the object. From that position, she can have jouissance of the Other in the man and from the phallus, even though, or possibly because, there is an absence of what was anticipated. And his own jouissance here concerns the object she has made of herself, and the phallus she imaginarily restores to him, because in renouncing the phallus conferred on him by the phallic function as universal, he can rediscover it on the inverted scale of her own jouissance.

This mode of jouissance has its place in the singularity of the sexual couple, outside of the law of discourse. It helps to lighten the burden of the absence of a relation of two in discourse, which is why it compensated for the alienation of the law for so long. The love that forms the basis of couples in this way contributes more generally to ensuring that the gap does not appear.

The two sexuated ways of responding to the gap between jouissances in the sexual relation have entirely different consequences. The masculine way, completely obedient to the system of the phallic function of the sexual law, functions through the process of carrying forward, and consequently the reversion of a jouissance to an identical state, by annulling and misrecognising its subtraction. The feminine way, which does not obey the phallic function of the sexual law completely, fabricates an imaginary phallic object according to a supplementary jouissance, in order to soften the impact of the subtraction. The flaw in the 'sexual relation' concerns both parties, but their individual failures are very different. One of them *a priori* fails to a greater extent than the other, but if he gives up on the phallic function of the law in order to link with the other's failure, they may achieve a relation together. These two sexuated positions and the possible relation between them are no longer anything other than references among others, and no longer carry the weight of the law.

This is how we can explain the difficulty of the 'sexual relation' for the man and the woman, and the way in which it may be surmounted. Starting with the same fact, each of their logics interprets it differently and responds accordingly. The man's way is to erase the failure of conjunction, creating complementary objects, surplus jouissance (*plus-de-jouir*), to block the gap, as discourse does universally. The way of a woman who develops a supplementary jouissance acknowledges the lack, and creates a knot in order to bind the couple together. So there is a beyond of the phallus available to both man and woman.

This feminine mode of jouissance, while objecting to the failure of the phallic function, does not denounce it, in the way that the logic of the hysteric may do by inscribing itself in it and repressing it. The feminine mode overcomes it without repressing it, and compensates for it without denying it. It acts at the point of disjunction in the sexual relation, creating something that can make it possible. When that succeeds, the man will himself participate in the other jouissance, where the castration he consents to is compensated for by the restitution accorded him through the symbol. In such a case he can very well situate himself 'in himself' according to the phallic function of discourse, in his personal and professional achievements, while also being 'for the Other', since he has given up the signifying phallus conferred on him by the law, and has jouissance of the phallic symbol that the woman's jouissance has restored to him and which, generally, is more reliable.

In the context of the second half of the last century, when sexual disjunction had exploded into the public domain in the works of the sexologists, and where it was constantly a question of explaining how one could arouse a woman to orgasm, and thus reduce the lack of conjunction, Lacan observed something entirely different. He considered that the question could not be resolved on the basis of orgasm, even if it was necessary to deal with it in those terms, but showed that sexual disjunction was not due solely to the effects of the sexual law. He also showed that a feminine jouissance could occur without orgasm, and could even make up for the lack of it. Orgasm is not aimed at as such, but may occur in some sense as a bonus.

VI. The road travelled since Freud

Freud had observed a defect in the relation between man and woman, since what he called 'the most common debasement in love life' consisted of, in men, a division between love without desire on the one hand, in a repetition of his love for the mother, and desire without love on the other, culminating in the desire for a prostitute. His description conjures up a kind of limping along, something that involved a kind of zig-zag. This is why Lacan could rightly say that what he called the absence of sexual relation was already hinted at in the Freudian text. Indeed, to say as Freud did that at the resolution of the Oedipus complex the affectionate and sensual current of early childhood is divided into two separate currents, and then that in adulthood they have trouble reuniting for fear of the incest that contaminates sexual jouissance, is already a satisfactory initial formulation of the sexual non-relation. It links this absence to the effects of the prohibition of incest, and the way they are subjectivised in the Oedipus complex; and these are very much the remit of psychoanalysis. But now we can see clearly that this is only one aspect of what is involved in the absence of the sexual relation.

The sexual law, according to the logic of the phallic function, also creates an object that preserves the man from the risk of incest, because by eliding the woman's jouissance it can avoid confronting him with it. Nonetheless, an object of this nature may also appear to have an incestuous aspect, since it orientates, or even prescribes a man's desire for a woman whom he has in some way engendered himself. The sexual law born of Genesis has the particularity of consisting in elaborating a schema that preserves an imaginary mode of incest, the maternal mode, while instituting another, the paternal one. It forbids one type of incest, while substituting for it a relation that evokes another type, broadly tolerated and even prescribed within this framework, and involving a perversion.

While the man flees insistently from anything that might evoke an incestuous jouissance of the other sex, desire for the woman he loves, or love for the woman he desires, the woman just as insistently seeks it out. These Freudian conceptions have largely retained their value, even though they are based on notions derived from the phallic function of the law. The latter no longer has the force of a universal law, but it remains the reference point in the unconscious both in cases of neurosis and beyond, according to the logic of the all-phallic. The 'sexual relation' in Lacan's sense could be defined entirely – in a first approximation – in Freudian terms, as whatever reunites the affectionate and sensual currents, thus articulating love and jouissance in the two partners. It would achieve 'this perfection that is imagined as the conjunction of two jouissances', involving love.

The masculine way and the feminine way of failing in the relation determine the only way of succeeding in it, taking little byways where there is no major highway marked out in discourse to find a route to approach the other sex. In what Lacan defined as the relation of the man to the feminine object a, we rediscover in part what Freud called the debasement of love life. When the man's desire is caused by an object of this type, by debasing an object held in high esteem, or in choosing a despised object, he is spared the incestuous aspect that may be taken on by the desire for the woman he loves. He may nonetheless love a phallic feminine object while also desiring her, but in that case his love is equivalent to a child's incestuous love. In these rather different cases, a man is not dealing with the other sex as such.

Freud made a first approach to the feminine mode of jouissance with the observation that prohibition (*l'interdit*) worked in its favour, but it was more a question of the *inter-dit*, in the sense of what cannot be a statement, but only a saying, since it stands in opposition to the expectations of the law of discourse. And, offering the man's phallic jouissance something other than the solitude of his complement, it enables the affectionate and the sensuous current to be reunited for both parties.

So Freud had identified a problem in the relation between man and woman, and had described it in terms of the anxiety around incest that haunts the sexual act. He quite rightly implied that in Judeo-Christian civilisation, the prohibition of sexual jouissance was linked to a certain contamination of sexuality through the prohibition of incest. In that culture, the woman's jouissance was assimilated to incest itself, through an extension of the prohibition way beyond its own borders. And this is what has disappeared with the erosion of the prohibition, leaving in its place a much clearer distinction between objects that really are incestuous and those which are only imaginarily so.

Freud did not envisage any other cause for the difficulty established at the heart of the relation of man and woman. But he had already reserved a place in the future of his theory, with his hypothesis of the biological 'rock' central to the principle of castration anxiety. And indeed, Lacan's taking up of this hypothesis opened up a whole new dimension in the causation of the sexual gap. While the considerable development of the relation between man and woman that has taken place since Freud's time has significantly reduced the impact of the sexual law, the retreat of the law has not fundamentally resolved the problem of the disjunction of the jouissances of man and woman, even if it has gone some way towards reducing it. Above all else, it has brought the problem to light. This new dimension of the conceptual development of psychoanalysis does not invalidate the fundamental role of the Oedipal organisation of the prohibition of incest, which creates a subject within the symbolic system, but it has shown how its scope is limited.

Lacan, in discovering this new sexual causality in the structures of the unconscious, opened up a dimension that cannot be seen as a consequence of the prohibition of incest, but can, conversely, explain its origin and its function. These new concepts are rooted not only in infancy, during which the tablets of stone on which the law prohibiting incest is written are put firmly in place, but later on in life when sexual relations occur. The phantasy of incest always hovers around the sexual act, but the reason for this is not simply the contamination of sexuality by its central prohibition; it is not due solely to the fact that the jouissance of a woman never ceases to evoke that of a mother. The incestuous phantasy can thus also be seen as having a function in relation to the fault in sexual union.

How do the consequences of the prohibition of incest interact with the logic constructed on the basis of the cut in the sexual act? On the basis of this question, we need to rethink the entire construction of our symbolic order, and this is much easier to grasp once the prohibition of sexual jouissance has disappeared, beyond incest itself.

Notes

1 Jacques Lacan, *Logic of the Phantasy*, seminar of 24 May 1967.
2 Lacan, *Anxiety*, op. cit., p. 262.
3 As Lacan puts it: 'The other pole of the signifier, its stopping action, is also there at the origin of the vocative of commandments'. Lacan, *Encore*, op. cit., p. 24.
4 This absence becomes visible as a hole, which is traumatic, and calls for some kind of invention. 'In the place where there is no sexual relation, there is traumatisation', as Lacan put it. 'One has to invent something. One invents what one can'. Jacques Lacan, *Les Non-dupes Errent*, seminar of 19 February 1974.
5 Jacques Lacan, *Logic of the Phantasy*, seminar of 1 March 1967.
6 Ibid.
7 This is the principle of causation proposed by Lacan in the seminar *Logic of the Phantasy*, ibid.
8 The reason the Borromean knot is so important for psychoanalysis stems from the fact that the symbolic order, such as it is constructed according to the phallic standard assigned to the Name of the Father, does not allow two sexes to be knotted together directly, so that their articulation can be achieved only through the intermediary of a third term, through this type of knot. For example, Lacan said that 'to the extent that we have to see the symbolic as removed from, subtracted from the One of phallic jouissance, the relation of bodies, as two, can only occur via the reference, to something that is other than the symbolic, which is distinct, that is, what of the three already appears in the most minimal writing'. Jacques Lacan, *Les Non-dupes Errent*, seminar of 21 May 1974.

Chapter 5

Organisation of the symbolic order

As we study these structures and logics, it no longer seems that the functioning of sex in human beings is conditioned solely by the fact that they speak and, in the sexual act, are subject to the effects of discourse and its laws. One particular biological aspect of this act, which we have isolated and highlighted, has always had, and continues to have, definitive consequences in the way the symbolic order that governs us is organised. A symbolic order is the whole gamut of signifiers, symbols, representations and logics constituted for a subject on the basis of what is transmitted to them through the family that influenced them, within the culture and the context they were born into, and what they made of it all and how they responded to it. The rapid development of discourse since the last century has unveiled the sexual structures, and allows us to draw conclusions about their effects based on Lacanian concepts that have gone virtually unnoticed in contemporary works on sexuality.

We have established that the phallus, as instrument of jouissance and power, is not just the signifier that transmits the law of the Father, but should also be considered as a signifier borrowed from a particularity of sexual biology, forming the basis of a certain grammar of discourse. As we saw earlier, Lacan, by drawing attention to this function, made an essential contribution to the development of Freud's concept of a biological 'rock', which he hypothesised in order to account for the importance of castration and the phallus in psychical life. The phallus is also based, perhaps primarily, on the cut in the sexual relation according to the law of pleasure, which represents a sort of commandment made flesh, leaving a gap open between the jouissances of the two sexes. Even though it does not appear, as it is masked by subjective satisfaction, this subtraction calls for a recovery of the lost jouissance in all sorts of forms of surplus jouissance, thus causing a process of desire. This is the essential pivot of the entire economy of objects, both phallic and other, that come into the place of a partner according to this modality.

If the symbolic order that governs us is partially based on this borrowing of a signifier from phallic jouissance, it follows that it will renew the gap that it induced between the psychical modes of jouissance of man and woman.[1] It involves an absence of the two of sex, for which it substitutes a sole one with its object *a*, and

DOI: 10.4324/9781003285984-6

on that basis symbolises an entire order of desire. No signifier can symbolise the hole that causes it to emerge and which it effaces. The phallus represents a pervasive solution that masks the subtraction as well as the disjunction of jouissances. By symbolising only one of them, the question of their conjunction is resolved. In the symbolic order, this determines an organisation that remains marked by the defect at the origin of its constitution.

The phallus is omnipresent in the symbolic order, even if only in latent form, because of its efficacy, but also because of this initial inefficacy. Why is it that the phallus, as signifier, is to be found everywhere in the unconscious, symbolising the attribute of the father, the desire of the mother, the subject and sexuation, and yet never where we expect it, at the point where it would allow the articulation of masculine and feminine jouissance, in discourse as well as in the sexual act? This is the reason: it is because it is not present to allow the articulation that it is present everywhere else. The symbolic order as a whole borrows its signifier from phallic jouissance, while eliding the jouissance that it struggles to attain. That is why it is marked by an even more radical absence of the two.

The effect of phallic signification in its entirety, of everything that involves having the phallus or not, being it or not, for an Other who either has it or not, is to mask the absence of the 'sexual relation' in the symbolic order. It organises the symbolisation of sexual difference between man and woman as a plus or a minus, a relation that is supposedly complementary, around the notion of the one's having it and the other's being it. Instead of an other as such, who counts as one, the subject connects to this object that constitutes a part of himself, completing the lost portion of his phallic jouissance. It is not counted as one, and the relation formed is not made up of two, but of 'one plus a', the numeric principle of this hierarchy. The symbolic order that is based on this 'one' of phallic jouissance then makes a cut through the articulation of the sexes, and thus reappropriates it.

We might think that the parental couple would nevertheless represent the 'two' of sex for the subject born of them, even though in our time the couple can take on multiple forms which may not necessarily add up to two, and may not involve two different sexes. For each child, the symbolic order is introduced through those who brought them into the world and take care of them; it is constructed along the lines of the Oedipus complex and the function of the Father. However, if we look carefully at the signifier of the Father, such as it has functioned from the beginnings of our Judaeo-Christian civilisation, we see that it does not introduce the two of sex either. This is what we now need to examine.

Until recently, psychoanalysis considered the phallic signifier as an attribute of the Father, indissociable from him. And yet it existed before the Name of the Father which, conversely, as we have seen, is actually based on the phallic signifier by giving to itself the function of regulating phallic jouissance; a total reversal! Examining this hypothesis will raise the question of what new dimensions this implies with regard to the fundamental law of the prohibition of incest, which is at its origin.[2]

I. Symbolic command of the biological 'rock'

Since the invention of psychoanalysis, we have known that the terms of the symbolic order within which the subject emerges stem from the succession of events relating to the Oedipus complex in childhood and their outcome, and that subjects inscribe themselves and participate according to the sexuation they choose. The child is immersed in this order well before actively subscribing to it. The reference to the symbolic Father that the child has to deal with depends on how its function is conceptualised in the community of discourse to which they belong, but it retains its mythical character, however it may have developed in a particular case.

Freud had proposed his myth of the Father of the 'primal horde' when he began to wonder about the origins of the prohibition of incest. He had attributed unlimited jouissance to this Father, while that of all the others was limited to the point of being confiscated. The limit concerned the number of women: the primordial Father was described as the only one who could have jouissance of all the women in the community, like the alpha male in certain animal species, and he, by doing this, confiscated the jouissance from all the other males, who were his sons. His murder by the sons was not, however, followed by unlimited jouissance for all of them, but by a self-imposed prohibition of having jouissance of the mothers, since that had been the prerogative of the Father. Paradoxically, the prohibition was derived from the extermination of the one who prohibited, and his all-embracing limit was transferred from the prohibition of jouissance to the prohibition of having jouissance of the mother. From this, Freud deduced the fundamental law of incest on the basis of a primitive drama of sexual jouissance concerning one man who limited the jouissance of all the others, while having no limits to his own.

This limit concerns the number of women he has jouissance of, but there is another fundamental limit inherent in sexual jouissance, the one we have discussed in terms of the limit of the pleasure principle. For the mythical Father, there is no limit to the number of women he may have, while phallic jouissance entails a limit of only one woman. At the point where Freud explored the origin of the prohibition of incest – what it means to have jouissance of all the women – Lacan pointed out that detumescence, as the incarnation of the limit of the sexual relation, with its symbolic system, stops a man from truly obtaining jouissance from one single woman. He considered that the statement 'having jouissance of all the women' was consequently the statement of an impossibility, since the particularity of his phallic jouissance made it impossible for a man to have jouissance, in the strict sense, of any woman. So he stated that 'having jouissance of all of them' was inconceivable, since it was 'already hard enough to be sufficient for one of them'.[3] And in any case this involved reversing 'having jouissance of' into 'making [them] have jouissance', which is not specified in the myth.[4]

The primal Father of the myth thus represents an all-powerful being in terms of having jouissance of all the women, and this by definition implies that he must be capable of having jouissance of a single one, of having the phallic jouissance of the sexual relation at his command, without any castration. He who can do the most can also do the least.

Commenting on this Freudian theorisation, Lacan emphasised its characteristic of being a neurotic phantasy, but did not challenge it as such, because in it he recognised precisely that which functions in the unconscious as the mythical Father of neurosis and of the community of discourses. This logic posits one exception who is not subject to any limit whatever where his jouissance is concerned, while all the others are limited, and on that basis the exception becomes the agent of the limit and of castration for all the others. By representing an impossibility as a possibility through being an exception, he is imagined as depriving all the others of sexual jouissance. This is Lacan's reading, in logical terms, of the myth of 'Totem and Taboo'.[5] In it he recognised a structure that is at work in human institutions, where privation is imposed on all concerned by one individual who is deprived of nothing and has jouissance without limits.

It can be stated like this: 'The fact that all men encounter a limit to their sexual jouissance is imputed to One alone who is responsible for it, being himself without any limits'. This sentence sums up the Freudian myth as it was translated into logic by Lacan. We may read this sentence taking the term of sexual jouissance in the sense of 'having jouissance of' all the women, as Freud formulated it. If we now read it again, without changing a single word, in the sense of the limit to each sexual act incarnate in the phallic cut, it takes on a completely different meaning. In reality, this proposition suggests both meanings: the limit of the number of women as well as the limit imposed on the act with one single woman.

So we propose a supplementary reading of the myth of 'Totem and Taboo' concerning the sexual act, according to the limit incarnated in detumescence and its effects. The myth of a Father who has jouissance of all the women is also the myth of a Father who has limitless jouissance in a single sexual act. This is what designates him as the agent of castration in both cases, in depriving the men of both women and phallic functionality.

Lacan did not mention this, and indeed he may not have thought it. But when he speaks of Freud's 'biological rock', referring to the materialisation of the limit of pleasure through detumescence, he designates a central process that necessarily intervenes in the construction of a primordial signifier of the Father who is immune to every form of castration. The Freudian myth accounts for the Father at work in the world of discourse and in neurosis, and can indeed be read as a phantasy. And since it represents a dream of limitless jouissance, it consists in denying not only the limit of 'having jouissance of' in the sense of possession, but also the limit of 'having jouissance' in the sense of turgidity. In practice, by denying the limit on the number of women a man may have jouissance of, it also denies, at least initially, the materialised limit on his jouissance with regard to only one woman. Having jouissance of 'all the women' implies by definition that he has jouissance of 'the whole woman'. This phantasy consists not only in crossing the limit, but in doubly subverting it, outbidding it; the act of denial is magnified when it concerns its mythical agent.[6] Not only does the limit not prevent him from having jouissance of a woman, but, raising the stakes through denial, it does not prevent him from having jouissance of all of them. The limit on phallic jouissance is denied to the power of two; this power is transformed into omnipotence. And we may even think that the number of women he is supposed to have jouissance of is all the greater in that it serves to deny the limit on a single sexual act, increasing the power of the denial of the limit regarding just one woman. Maybe this is where the structural justification for polygamy is to be found.

This can be linked with Lacan's interpretation of Genesis, where God metaphorically commands the subtraction, and thus the limit of the sexual act, and from this he derived the sexual law[7] in terms of a 'simple initial recognition'[8] of this functioning of the object that emerges from the sexual cut as a force aiming to refind an equivalent of the subtracted jouissance through phantasy. This is where the naming of God as the agent of this function springs from, that there should be an agent of the subtraction, where there is only the subject of the unconscious enmeshed in language, the biology of his organ, and his relation to the jouissance of the other: that there should be one who governs the law of pleasure, who is responsible for the relation of the subject to the jouissance of the woman, together with its non-conjunction and elision.

In the same way as the myth of the primal Father being responsible for the privation of jouissance for everyone else confiscates all the women, the myth of Genesis confiscates woman by substituting this object. In the sexual act the man is subject to the limit imposed by God, and he in turn imposes it on his partner, as a remainder of the subtraction. It is a way for him to abdicate his own responsibility for the scansion of the sexual act to this God, of 'saving his phallic bacon [*retirer son épingle phallique du jeu*]'.[9] Lacan concluded that such a God is useless,[10] but we know that there were to be a number of changes in his thinking regarding this question. At this point a hierarchal chain is created that brings meaning to a halt, substituting itself for an absent conjunction that generates no meaning at all.

Similarly, the Name of the Father is the one for whom the mother occupies the function of object *a*, and she herself has this object in the form of her child. At this point the hierarchical chain continues, in the relation of one single individual with their object as a part of themselves. It too creates a relation of 'one plus *a*', and not of two. Nor does what takes the place of the 'sexual relation' according to the law articulate the two, any more than does the Father. This is why, according to Lacan, he has a quality of 'perversion', which in a punning way is called 'père-version' (*père = father*), which is the paradoxical source of its efficacy. There is no structure fundamental to the symbolic order that includes the two of sex. Because of the very construction of these fundamental signifiers – the phallus borrowed from the jouissance of the penis, with its cut, and the Father nominated as its agent – the symbolic order could not possibly include it. So we can see that the function of the Father, at another level, engenders the same particularity as the phallus, and that it is likewise unable to determine a relation between the sexes that would add up to two.

Nor is there a phallus to castrate in the sexual act, because the phallus is there only to fend off anxiety; and nor is there a Father to kill, because he is there to bear the responsibility for the phallic limit. The aim of the Freudian myth of the Father of the horde was to explain the origin of the prohibition of incest, closely bound up with the symbolic order, through the killing of a primal Father and then the implementation of his law. On that basis, we may wonder if the biological 'rock' of castration also played a part in the construction of the prohibition of incest.

II. The function of suppleance of the prohibition of incest

If the myth of 'Totem and Taboo' suggests the possibility of a latent and supplementary meaning regarding the impact of the limit of sexual jouissance in the construction of the symbolic order, we may wonder if a re-reading of it might shed new light on the law of the prohibition of incest, since its aim was to explain its origins.[11]

The law of the pleasure principle regulates all jouissances, by forbidding them to go beyond a certain threshold, but this is only materialised biologically in the case of sexual jouissance through detumescence. This particular characteristic was obviously borrowed in order to create a symbolic law of the phallus in the double sense of the genitive: the law it imposes and the law to which it submits. We have seen the various elements and the ways in which they have been taken up. In this case, there would be no reason to go beyond the prohibition of incest, since a law that is partially natural, even though it has been interpreted in terms of a cut, contributed to it. And yet, human sexual jouissances are widely symbolised on the basis of the prohibition of incest guaranteed by the Father. We may wonder why this is.

Lacan, when faced with this question, argued initially that sexual jouissance only had the prohibition, applied to the body itself, as a reference: in other words, the law of the pleasure principle.[12] And indeed, it is only in terms of a limit that it is to be found in the unconscious and its formations. However, this fundamental law of the subject, which regulates jouissance according to a limit, and has a mortal jouissance as its horizon, in reality concerns only the body of the individual and not that of the other. Since it structures only the jouissance of the body in which it resides, it could not possibly apply itself as a law governing sexual jouissance, which also involves another body. So, he deduces, it connects with sexual jouissance only in referring the law of the pleasure principle to another body, that of the mother. This is the essential point: the prohibition of incest, which as a general rule only limits the pleasure of the individual's own body, is in fact extended onto another body, the one from which it emerged.

However, we find that the sexual relation is precisely an area where the limit of the pleasure principle is imposed not only on the individual's own body but also on that of the other. Within the order of the drives, this is a completely exceptional phenomenon. In the sexual relation, the man's limit of pleasure is indeed imposed on the woman he penetrates, because the cut in the functionality of the penis interrupts the sexual act for both partners in the couple. Lacan did not make much of this point, as if it went without saying, and without a doubt it does go without saying. Does this mean that if the limit of pleasure is valid for two bodies the other body is a part of the individual's own body? Certainly, as we have emphasised earlier, what is symbolised by this limit of phallic jouissance can only be the basis for autoerotic jouissance, as is implied in the metaphor of Genesis, where the woman is formed as a part of the man's body. Hence it is necessary to approach it via the prohibition of incest in order to reconnect with the dimension of the two of sex. The omnipresence of incest and its prohibition in the unconscious stems from the fact that it symbolises a relation of the subject with an other as such, in other words, a two of sex, and that it is unique in so doing. And yet it does not symbolise anything other than what should not take place, and not the way in which it actually could take place in the psychical economy. As Lévi-Strauss pointed out, it symbolises it only in the way that prohibiting certain women entails prescribing others.

But from that point on, how does this fundamental prohibition develop?

I left this question hanging in 2004,[13] but let us now try to answer it. First of all, let us recall that there is another fundamental case in which the law of the regulation of pleasure of one body is imposed on another body, where it is valid for both. This is the case of the mother, whose limit of pleasure with regard to the bodily drives is imposed on the child, first in the womb, then as her baby, since it is she who controls the withdrawal of the breast, although the latter is voluntary, whereas detumescence is not. So, with the sexual relation, we find there are two exceptions to the functioning of the pleasure principle, in the sense that they are the only cases where a limit of jouissance of one individual's body is imposed on that of another, where the limit affects two bodies rather than one alone. These exceptions are essential, since in a way they constitute the only laws of pleasure that are imposed biologically on another body. A law that has an impact on the body while imposing itself on another body is a law that has the power to borrow characteristics through the language that symbolises the conjunction of bodies.

We find that these limits that are valid for two bodies are imposed in an inverse direction in the two cases respectively, where the two sexes are concerned. The mother's limit of pleasure in breast-feeding is imposed in the direction of the younger generation, from a mother to her sons, so in this case, from feminine to masculine. On the other hand, where the sexual relation is concerned, the limit of pleasure is imposed by the man on the woman, with the detumescence that brings the act to an end. In both cases, the limits are imposed as if the other's body were part of the individual's own, in an autoerotic mode. In the course of a human life, these two laws succeed one another in a circular fashion, one taking the place of the other, when sons and daughters escape from the maternal law of pleasure in order to enter into that of the sexual relation, and then themselves procreate, and so on.

If a logic were to be derived from this, it would mean that the incestuous relation would be what confronted each of these two exceptions to the law of pleasure, going against the grain of the way life unfolds. This relation is the one where the limit of the man's pleasure would be imposed on the woman who bore him, and thus would invert the law: it would abolish the succession from one limit to the next in the diachronicity of a life; it would entail the abolition of all logic. The incestuous relation represents the essence of what is immediately considered reprehensible as soon as the first stone of the symbolic order is laid. It constitutes the contrary intersection of the two symbolisations that make up the laws of pleasure, the forbidden point of exception, where the one and the other confront each other and cancel each other out. It is by definition excluded as soon as the first human symbolisations get hold of the biological particularities of the body in order to create laws according to these logics.

In ancient Greek societies, we find descriptions of a circular logic in filiation and transmission where, generation after generation, the same cycles were repeated with the same milestones, and the same identities recurred, with the grandson reincarnating the grandfather, etc.[14] It was described as being contemporary with the prehistoric mother-goddess cults, with their myths of incest taking place and then being punished, with young gods considered to be the resulting sons. This may echo a logic borrowed from the laws of pleasure: first the mother's logic was imposed, until that of the sexual relation was substituted for it, and the man's logic was imposed in the sexual act. When this relation led to procreation, the cycle would pass the same point once again, reproducing itself in a circular way between one system and the other.[15] It would be interrupted by the establishment of the patrilineal system, and the passage into the age of classical Greece, when the linear logic of a signifier of the Father was substituted for the circular logic.

Greco-Roman civilisation adopted the second logic, according to the law that imposed itself on the sexual relation, of man and woman. In order for this to happen, the one to whom the subtraction that limited the sexual relation was attributed would also be the procreator, substituted for the mother. In this case there is no circularity – given the passage from the law of the pleasure of the mother to that of the sexual relation, and thence to procreation – but rather a distinct and definitive linearity. The function of procreation becomes paternal, and its agent assumes the two laws of pleasure. If the Father is posited as both procreator and the agent of the regulation of the relation – in other words he condenses the two functions – then the function of Father will always allow the symbolic system, based on the logic of the sexual relation, and therefore of the phallus, to operate in a linear fashion.[16]

The God of the Bible brought about a metaphor of this order. The Jewish invention of this God established the Name of the Father as agent of the subtraction that regulates the sexual relation, compensated for by the feminine phantasy object, and mankind submitted to this God. Later on, the function of Father was attributed to him. Even nowadays, the rite of circumcision shows which organ is concerned in reality, according to the divine rule of Genesis. This pact consecrates the God responsible for the subtraction that limits the sexual relation, by dedicating the subtraction of each new foreskin to him.

All this suggests that symbolisation based on the limit of the sexual relation was taken up by monotheism, which made itself the agency of sexual law. And this is why, to bring about its completion, the prohibition of incest was as radical and as widespread as it was, since it symbolised the sexual relation as being only autoerotic, the other body being a part of one's own. Moses made himself distinct from the law of the Egyptians, with his horror of incest.[17]

Egypt, that other great civilisation, had indeed endowed incest with a sacred status, not through punishing its practice between goddesses and their sons, but in prescribing it as a right, even a sacred duty, of the pharaohs, in the name of the transmission of the royal blood between brothers and sisters, fathers and daughters. We may well think that the royal exception, which allows the practice of incest, serves as an agent for prohibiting it for everyone else, according to the logic described above in relation to the primal Father. In this case, too, the prohibition of incest serves to symbolise the sexual relation and is added to the limit of pleasure that symbolises only an autoerotic jouissance.

Our own Judaeo-Christian history made quite a different use of these logics of pleasure to that of the ancient East. For example, the ancient East prescribed the retention of 'the seed' with the aim of 'ecstasy', clearly in order to overcome the detumescence that follows ejaculation. As for monotheism, it made the terminal phallic subtraction into a law, the law of Yahweh, of God and of Allah. And sexual laws everywhere have adopted a grammar that cuts into the articulation of the sexes so that only one is retained, according to the phallic signifier, whether faced with a single feminine object or a number of them.

By presenting their law of the relation of the sexes as a law of nature, while in our century it has proved to be a problematic construction of civilisation, the patriarchal civilisations and their monotheistic religions have in one sense spoken the truth, but not in the sense they might have intended. If this law was constituted on the basis of the natural law of detumescence, it did so by eliding the other side of jouissance, and that is not natural.

III. The effect of discourse on sex, and of sex on discourse

So strictly speaking there are not two sexes in the symbolic order, but a single one organised as two poles and two bodies, around the third term, the phallus. According to the sexual law, the sexual relation is symbolised only as a relation of being to having, which has nothing sexual about it, and defines something other than a relation between two sexes. The function of discourse is closely linked with the phallic function that is deployed within it.[18] The major concept of the unconscious, which the symbolic order borrows from phallic jouissance[19] – in the concrete limit that it involves – radicalises the disjunction between the sexes that it operates in the sexual act in the grammar of discourse. The entire order of desire and of the law is thus derived from a fictional structure centred on the signifier that underpins this jouissance, and on the significations that it engenders. This is why Lacan was able to deduce that language as a whole is positioned in the space of this sexual gap, and this proves the fundamental difference between what would be a 'sexual relation' and the sexual law that takes its place.[20]

To this extent, the phallus may be called the cause of language, because in creating an obstacle to the 'sexual relation', it calls upon language to deal with the gap. It may seem surprising to present it as an obstacle, since the erect penis is what enables the sexual relation, in the everyday sense of the expression, to take place. But as we have argued, this complicates matters both at the level of biology and in the symbolic register. We would do better to speak of the cause, rather than the origin, of language, since the origin as such is inaccessible to us. Moreover, we are examining two orders of causality that have an inverse relation to one another, even if they are impossible to dissociate. The gap in the 'sexual relation' exists because language exists, but we might also propose that language exists because there is the gap that language allows us to deal with.

In psychoanalysis, then, causality consists in a double interaction between sex and language, and it can only be grasped in this way. It bears on the central concept of the 'sexual relation' in its link with language, in both directions. When Lacan tells us that he refuses to become involved in any question of origins, and that one might just as well say that discourse begins with the fact that there is a sexual gap, as the other way round,[21] he implies that it would be impossible to determine a single causality. The sexual non-relation is certainly produced because language exists, and thus because of its law prohibiting incest, as Freud began to discover, but conversely, as Lacan added, the sexual disjunction gave rise to the grammar of discourse that radicalises it. And he was right to insist on this, since according to where one positions oneself, there is indeed an inverse causality. If one positions oneself at the level of a subject, which is the ontogenetic level, the Oedipal unconscious imprints its mark and its absence of the two of sex in discourse. But at the other pole, that of phylogenesis, which is that of civilisation, sexual laws borrow the phallic subtraction as symbolisation in order to give up on the articulation of the two, by eliding one of the two sexes. The two modes of causality are therefore both true, and are joined in this complex topology.

Lacan did not leave the question of the origin of language entirely untouched, however, since he created a fiction in the form of a hypothesis. Language was supposed to have been born out of the very function of detumescence as the limit of the sexual act. This is how he put it:

> Detumescence in the male has generated the special type of appeal that is spoken language, by virtue of which the necessity of speaking is introduced into its dimensions. It's from this that logical necessity as grammar of discourse arises. You can see that this is pretty thin![22]

What was the point of creating a fiction about the origin of language in this way, given that in truth there is nothing that can possibly be said about it? It has the same point as any fiction, as any myth, either in psychoanalysis or elsewhere. When confronted with a point in the real that cannot be articulated in its entirety on the basis of discourse, a fiction fulfils the role of fixing a meaning, because the real has no meaning. And meaning, once fixed in this way, allows the aporia that has been circumscribed not to be overlooked. It is impossible to decide between the terms of the alternative: 'Does the gap in the sexual relation exist because of discourse, or is it because the gap exists that discourse exists?', but it is hardly an inconsequential matter whether one is privileged over the other or not. This fiction allows us to observe that how we approach the question is not a matter of indifference. In this sense, in the beginning was not the Word but the lack of conjunction in the sexual relation, in terms of a subtraction that summons up the Word.

The metaphor of Genesis established the logical schema of a sexual law that lasted more than two millennia. It did so on the basis of sexual jouissance, accompanying it with the literal commentary, 'they shall be of one flesh', which was applied in a very particular sense since only one sex was involved with regard to their desire. It was based on a subtraction, the value of which was carried forward onto a feminine object, instead of articulating two jouissances. In so doing, it echoed one of the facts of nature, which does not need the conjunction of two jouissances in order to achieve fertilisation, which gives jouissance along with fertilisation, rather than the other way round, accompanied by the message 'Go forth and multiply', which shows that the choice was made in favour of procreation to the detriment of jouissance. The meaning produced by this system of phallic signification is indeed effective in allowing human beings to copulate and reproduce the species, in a far more continuous way than animal instinct. The race has not become extinct within this framework, and from this point of view 'God's sexual blunder'[23] involves a definite skilfulness where fertility is concerned.

So two orders of causality operate between sex and language. For each subject, sexuation is constructed via their own particular Oedipal pathway under the effect of language, conditioned by castration and phallic signification, and symbolising the sexual relation through the prohibition of incest. But the relation between the sexes also results from what has been borrowed by the symbolic order from phallic jouissance and its limit. The different orders of causation are distinct and yet are superimposed on one another to the extent of being practically impossible to tell apart at any given moment. In the singularity of the sexual encounter, all these elements converge in the face of whatever real emerges.

From the point of view of the history of civilisation, the symbolic order developed according to religions and ideologies that produced sexual laws on the basis of the phallic function that constitutes an obstacle to the 'sexual relation'. For each subject born into the order of language, castration initially results in the symbolic subtraction of incestuous jouissance, according to the Oedipus complex and the function of the Father, and the subject responds according to an unconscious choice. But each sexual encounter entails the same real, a biological threshold in relation to which the law has adopted or excluded certain aspects in order to create itself. In psychoanalysis one can no longer consider that it is only the signifying system that organises sex in a univocal way, because the inverse incidence of sex on language operates just as much by providing the law of discourse with signifiers. And there is no point in trying to decide which of them came first.

Ordinarily, something that is the consequence of something else cannot also be its cause; and yet from this point of view it is the case, and in order to grasp it we need to resort to a particular topology. The figure known as the interior eight can be made very easily by crossing over an elastic band, thus forming an eight which can then be folded over with one loop on top of the other, so that they appear to merge, and it is no longer possible to determine which had logical precedence.[24] But if you pull on one of the loops, they separate, one becoming larger and more external, the other smaller and internal, and we can then see clearly how they are linked to one another, being neither equivalent nor symmetrical.

So the absence of 'sexual relation' in the symbolic order is certainly a product of discourse, since it states a sexual law that elides one sex and does not create a relation of two between them, but the grammar of discourse itself is formed on the basis of a primary split between their jouissances. Each subject approaches the sexual act according to whatever has resulted from the Oedipus complex for them, and from the position they have taken up in it, but they still encounter a gap between the jouissances of the sexual couple, which is both the result and a cause. This is what caused it at its very origin, although that origin cannot possibly be known.

The causality between sex and language, then, is double and inverse, and there is no need to make a choice when we wonder whether it is because man speaks that 'there is no sexual relation', or whether man speaks because there is none.[25] The two facets of the question cannot be dissociated from one another, each is causally related to the other, and it does not matter which came first in this instance, whereas it does matter if we are to understand the question in its entirety. While castration for the child comes before any effect of language, the entry into the field of the sexual act places each individual at the intersection of this causal chain.

There is thus a real heterogeneity between the subject who is situated outside the field of the sexual act, whether a child or an adult without sexuality, and the one who enters into the field of the sexual act, positioning themself at the intersection of the two facets. The subject who engages with this field encounters the real of sex at the same time as its symbolic and imaginary constructions. The child does not perceive the gap in the articulation of the sexes other than in the difficulties in the parents' relation. Adolescence marks the entry into this field, between the last stumblings of the Oedipus complex and the first impasses of the 'sexual relation'. The adults who exclude the sexual act from their existence close off what can be revealed by it. The subject who plunges into the field of the sexual act is constantly confronted with its consequences, with its revelations of the real, with the hope of making a One, with its obstacle to the relation in the form of phallic jouissance; and yet nonetheless with the subjective satisfaction that predominates.

IV. The logical background to contemporary developments

A symbolic order is by definition in a constant state of development, in an ontogenetic way, concerning a subject from the moment of birth, and in a phylogenetic way from its foundation within a civilisation to its current state. However, the speed or the visibility of the development and of the alterations it entails do not always go at the same pace. Within both a civilisation and an individual's life, there may be periods of apparent stasis, and others – following latent alterations that may have passed unnoticed – in which there are upheavals that seem to shake an entire logic to its very core. Our own Western civilisation went through such an upheaval in the second half of the last century, and it appears now as if everything had suddenly changed, in the sexual relation as well as in the social link between the sexes. It is too early to grasp in its entirety what has happened, or what has followed from it, but it is possible to discern some of its logical principles.

In certain fundamental dimensions, lines have shifted, borders have been moved, some have disappeared, and others are being redrawn. The logic of discourse emanated from a universal functioning where one law was imposed on all, male and female, in the name of one exception who escaped it. Apart from a few communities with limited discourses which have regrouped to apply it in certain regions, the logic that is entirely based on the phallic function is nowadays only one reference among others: it no longer has the force of law, and the relation of its subject to his 'other half' is no longer the only reference.

In 1973[26] when Lacan showed the two modes of logic operative in the masculine and the feminine, he was defining nothing other than what was in the process of happening in the development of our society. On the one hand, we find the phallic function with its castration and its exception, the Father, who commands the phallus, the logic of the all-phallic that defines both masculine logic and that of neurosis. Within this framework, each particular case can be based only on the universal, in order to satisfy the rule, or to identify with the exception. In addition to this, as we have seen, another logical mode was worked out, which does not refer to the universal, does not form the basis of a rule for everyone, and is not derived solely from the phallic function. Its relation to castration can only be defined one by one, because there is no exception that governs everyone else's. It is not a logic of the subject of the phantasy, but rather of an object that lends itself to the phantasy of the other while deploying its own desire with regard to the phallus. In order to be defined, it demands to be liberated from traditional logics, because it remains outside of discourse, or constitutes a discourse without speech, like the psychoanalytic discourse. While this logic has always existed, it has gained ground in contemporary developments in our symbolic order. Partially doing without the function of the Name of the Father that is the basis of the universal and the all-phallic, it has become more prominent since Western societies have undergone a significant weakening of religious and patriarchal beliefs, and have embarked upon a deconstruction of this fundamental signifier.

Contemporary experience includes this logic of the phallic function in a way that is now universally limited and circumscribed, or is just one reference among others. And on the other hand, in a unary way, in a logic of the particular, we find this sort of inversion of the status of the object with many modes of elaboration of the two in the sexual couple. This is the first aspect of what we can observe in contemporary developments.

The other major aspect of these alterations is implicit in the first one, and concerns the slippage of the frontiers of sex as such, compared with the way it was previously organised. Whereas the logics at work used to separate subjects universally into one sex, and objects into the other – according to the discourse of one sex and the being outside discourse of the other – the frontier between the sexes was drawn in terms of discourse, marriage, kinship and power. The institutions of language had resolutely stamped their marks on sex according to the logic of the phallic function. There were two major factors which probably caused this to happen, at the birth of our civilisation, as a sort of emergency. One concerned the need for the development of the logos, the logics and symbolic constructions of human institutions, in the millennia before out time. The current acceleration of the productions of the discourse of science is no longer determined to the same extent by the logos, by discourse, but by its literal productions, in particular its mathematical writings. The other factor concerned the necessary development of the populating of our planet, and probably the Church Fathers, the founders of Christianity, had understood that the phallic cut in the sexual relation satisfied the aim of procreation even if it did not satisfy the conjunction of jouissances, and therefore jouissance as such. By choosing the renunciation of jouissance that consisted in defining the sexual relation as destined only for procreation, Christianity in its origins privileged the priorities of its time, and adopted a logic that corresponded to these to achieve its aims.

At the present time in our civilisation, when an urgent need to populate the Earth is no longer on the agenda, but rather the question of overpopulation, and when the march of humanity towards the construction of institutions is no longer central compared to their regular reorganisation, something entirely different is happening. And thanks to the dwindling belief in the Christian God, the primacy of jouissance, which had been pushed aside, is re-emerging. As for the relation between the sexes, it appears that discourse could designate them only in an artificial way, as a fiction, and that the subject of speech is not sexuated as such. The jouissance belonging to the subject, known as phallic jouissance, is no longer the domain of one sex but of both. Women have broadly invested in phallic jouissance, which is now accessible to them in all registers.

It is no longer possible to describe the logic and the jouissance of men and of women respectively in a symmetrical way. The subject who obeys the phallic function completely is masculine, whatever their sex. Phallic jouissance is made of the one libido which is no more masculine than it is feminine, but rather neutral or asexual, and animates the subjectivity of the speaking being. Whoever participates both in this function and in the other jouissance is feminine.

The massive redistribution of sexuated elements is a response to the developments in a society that can now partially do without some of its fundamental logics. The subject is today determined between the logic of the phallic function, which is still operative at the level of everyone's social achievements, and that of sex, where, in each carnal encounter, the subject is sustained as such, or lends themself to being the object.

V. The mythical father of the unconscious at the heart of the sexual act

In the course of these reflections, we have seen the extent to which the function of the mythical Father drives deep roots into the heart of the processes of the unconscious, indeed far more so than we thought. The involvement of the God of the Bible in the cut in the act and in the relation of the sexes matches his massive presence in the imaginary and symbolic formations of the unconscious. The mythical primal Father, to whom Freud attributed the traits of the Father of the horde, who had jouissance without limits, and created limits for all the others, is the very source of this one God, who restores his rights to him. While belief in him may have dwindled in the Christian West, the unconscious power of the mythical Father remains intact, as an imaginary figure who proscribes the phallic cut in the sexual relation.

This cut, which is just as present for women as for men – even though they are in a position to free themselves from it and work out their own singular pathway within each sexual couple – still makes its presence felt at the heart of the sexual act. For a woman, it combines the Father who once inspired her Oedipal love, liberating her from maternal alienation, the Father of adolescence who was supposed to desire her incestuously in order to initiate her into womanhood, who has all the women at his disposal as well as all of one woman, this Father of the sexual relation who could bring her unimaginable jouissance if it were not prohibited. But a woman's jouissance takes the step of giving this up, finishing with this belief, developing her desire by going beyond the sexual law that he embodied. For a man, the mythical Father combines the Father who forbade his Oedipal love, the Father of adolescence who supposedly desired him, since he has jouissance of all males as well as all females, and then the Father of the sexual relation who has control of his organ, of his jouissance and his detumescence, which determines his castration. This is why the Father is to be found in the formations of the unconscious, dreams and phantasies, driving its roots into the sexual act through all these different functions.

Notes

1 This is Lacan's argument in *Les Non-dupes Errent*, seminar of 21 May 1974.
2 This chapter was published as an article, 'Nouvelles remarques sur la loi de l'interdit de l'inceste', *Figures de la psychanalyse*, No. 30, Toulouse, Érès, October 2015.

3 Here we can quote the whole of the fragment referred to: 'No psychology of this original father is conceivable. However, in the way in which it is presented it evokes derision . . . he who enjoys all the women is inconceivable to imagine, whereas it is fairly normally observable that it is already hard enough to be sufficient for one of them. We are referred here to a completely different reference, that of castration, as soon as we have defined it as the principle of the master signifier'. *The Other Side of Psychoanalysis*, op. cit., p. 124, translation modified.

4 Unless we define 'having jouissance of' as being precisely that which consists in 'making [them] have jouissance'; the signification is not fixed as such, since it involves two distinct modalities of the phallus, as we have described earlier. Freud clearly evoked the signifying process in his myth, 'the one who has all the women', whereas its signification can slide around in the imaginary so that it becomes 'the one who makes them have jouissance'.

5 This reading is found especially in the seminar *D'un discours qui ne serait pas du semblant*, ed. J-A Miller, Paris, Seuil, 2006.

6 This is similar to the interpretation implicit in the work of the philosopher Paul Audi, *Le théorème du Surmâle, Lacan selon Jarry*, Paris, Verdier, 2011, p. 134. We have already commented on this in 'Partition du sexe et de l'amour', *Figures de la psychanalyse*, No. 23, Toulouse, Érès, 2012.

7 A commentary can be found in Gisèle Chaboudez, 'La réalité sexuelle', *Che Vuoi?*, No. 29, 2008. This commentary needed to be brought up to date and extended, and that is what has been done in the present work.

8 Jacques Lacan, *L'acte psychanalytique*, seminar of 21 February 1968.

9 As Lacan put it: 'This rut of the Name of the Father, of the Father as naming, emerged in the Bible . . . and is for man a way of saving his phallic bacon'. Jacques Lacan, *RSI*, seminar of 11 March 1975.

10 'This tribal God is just the rather useless complement . . . which gives the partner lacking to the asexual body of man. Lacking in what way? Because he is "apphlicted" with a phallus which is what blocks for him the jouissance of the body of the Other'. Ibid.

11 This idea, first explored in 2004 in my *Rapport sexuel et rapport des sexes*, Paris, Denoël, 2004, p. 263 *et seq.*, is expanded on here.

12 'In other words, sexual jouissance only borrows its structure from the prohibition of jouissance applied to one's own body, that is to say, at the very precise halting point and frontier where it becomes mortal jouissance. And it only joins the sexual dimension in making the prohibition bear on the body that gave birth to one's own body, that is, the mother's body. It's only this way that what introduces the law, that is sexual jouissance, can be structured and reached in discourse. The actual partner can at times be reduced to one, but not any one, the one who gave birth to you'. Lacan, *D'un discours qui ne serait pas du semblant*, op. cit., pp. 107–8.

13 In Chaboudez, *Rapport sexuel et rapport des sexes*, op. cit.

14 Notably in *Dionysos*, by Maria Daraki, commented on in my *Le concept du phallus*, Paris, Lysimaque, 1995.

15 Our unconscious logic of alienation-separation also involves, if on a different basis, a continuous circularity.

16 However, in Greek religious mythology in which the passage to patrilineality took place, far from submitting to the Fathers, the sons castrated them.

17 These reflections are explored in Gisèle Chaboudez, 'Les Noms de l'Un tout seul, les nombres du rapport sexuel', paper given at the Journées d'Espace analytique, *Le psychanalyse et le fait religieux*, 19 and 20 March 2016, *Figures de la psychanalyse*, 34, 2017, Toulouse, Érès.

18 This link is also emphasised in other terms in the works of Jacques Derrida, and is named phallogocentrism.

19 The thesis we are exploring here and will develop throughout the present work is evoked by Lacan in the following quote: '[T]his signifier is in some sense removed, subtracted, borrowed from phallic jouissance itself, and it is to the extent that the signifier is the substitute that the signifier itself comes to block what it is that can't be written, that I call the sexual rapport'. Lacan, *Les Non-dupes Errent*, op. cit., seminar of 21 May 1974. This takes on all its force if we take into account the chain of causes discussed previously.

20 We will quote the text in full here, since it constitutes the main thesis that we are interpreting: 'What I propose is this . . . that language has its field set out in the gap of the sexual rapport that the phallus leaves open. What it introduces is not two terms that define male and female, but the choice between terms that have a very different nature and function, which are called "being" and "having". What proves this, what sustains this, and what makes this distance absolutely clear and definitive, is – and this has not been noticed – the substitution of what's called the sexual law for the sexual relation. This is where the distance is, where there is nothing in common between, on the one hand, what can be said about a relation which would constitute a law to the extent that it is based on, in whatever form, an application that is close to a mathematical function, and, on the other, a law which is coherent with the whole register of what we call desire and prohibition. It's from the very gap of prohibition that the conjunction, even the identity, of desire and the law derives. Correlatively, everything that derives from the effect of language, anything that establishes the "demansion" of truth, has the structure of fiction'. Lacan, *D'un discours qui ne serait pas du semblant*, op. cit., p. 68. The identity noted here between desire and the law should not be understood as a desire conforming to the law, as Foucault understood it, and consequently found it quite astonishing, but rather as a law that has been worked out in conformity with an unconscious desire.

21 Ibid., p. 107.

22 Jacques Lacan, *Or Worse, The Seminar of Jacques Lacan, Book XIX*, ed. J-A Miller, Cambridge, Polity, 2018, pp. 37–48.

23 An expression cited and commented on by Jacques Derrida, *Artaud le Moma*, Paris, Galilée, 2002, p. 22.

24 The interior eight or double loop is the topological writing Lacan used to indicate, for example, what is at stake in the transference in *The Four Fundamental Concepts of Psychoanalysis*, London, Routledge, 1977, p. 271.

25 This is how we should interpret the way Lacan put it: 'The relation of man and woman as distinct, from inhabiting language, has made a statement of this relation. Is it the absence of this relation that exiles them in their *stabitat*? Is it from inhabiting it that the relation can only be inter-dicted {inter-dit}?' *L'Etourdit*, Scilicet 4, Paris, Seuil, 1973, p. 11.

26 See Lacan, *Encore*, op. cit., p. 78.

Chapter 6

How the sexuated logics may be knotted together

The events of the last century showed us clearly that the sexual law organising the social links between the sexes did not form the basis for a relation of two: the reality of Lacan's curious aphorism was shown to be at work throughout society as a whole. From the 1970s onwards, he would state that there is no 'sexual relation' that can be written, in the sense that discourses would be able to express a relation of two sexes. To be written means both to be expressed in a discourse or a universal law, and to be written mathematically as a proportion.

There is certainly a relation that establishes a proportion, which the law establishes by making the feminine object a part of the masculine subject, i.e. the '*a*' and its relation to the 'one', but it is not sexual as such. There is certainly a relation that can be called sexual as soon as two desires are involved, rather than just one, with their logics and their jouissances, but it cannot be written in discourse; it is the wordless discourse of supplementary, feminine jouissance. Lacan's formulation does not constitute a curse, but rather a rigorous observation of the state of the institutions of language as regards sex. The articulation chosen between two partners is valid only for themselves, and does not even constitute a law for them, since it can easily be undone. In an era when the universal no longer has any force of law concerning sexuation and the social link between the sexes, it is important for us to grasp how this mode of relation operates, since it is not inscribed within a universal law, but springs from a choice and an act made by two people together.

I. The two sexuated logics

Lacan's work on sexuated logics was an extension of Freud's theory, and enabled the modes of jouissance and desire of each sex to be clarified, as well as their possible articulation. One of these logics, the masculine, can be recognised in the discourse of sexual law, in the form of the phantasy and the phallic function, and the other, the feminine, lends itself to the phantasy, but is only constituted as such outside discourse. They bring a new dimension to psychoanalytic theory – and specifically Freudian theory – which up to that point had concerned only what functioned within the register of discourse, and so could not truly approach the

DOI: 10.4324/9781003285984-7

core of feminine logic and supplementary jouissance, since it only described the feminine from the masculine point of view.

Since the earliest days of psychoanalysis, conceptual descriptions have evolved significantly. When Freud began to formulate the unconscious terms of femininity and masculinity, the contemporary relation between the sexes within the social bond was said to exist as a law of 'nature'. However, Freud did not hesitate to designate it as a development that was symptomatic of civilisation, since he considered neurotic organisations such as hysteria and obsession to reflect the stated norms of femininity and masculinity, and this had a considerable impact on further developments in the field.

When Lacan took up the question again in 1956, he began to describe the sexual law as a construction around the phallic signifier and its signification, in which, he said, the woman is contained in a position 'of a signifier, or even of a fetish'.[1] This observation had been expressed in plenty of other places outside of psychoanalysis, in the movements and thinking of the feminists, and later in queer and gender studies,[2] where gender, as something elaborated by society, was definitively differentiated from anatomical sex. Lacan's formulation, as we have seen, added that the omnipresence of the phallic system, both in the unconscious and in the institutions of language, is substituted for a relation between the sexes that their two jouissances cannot create in any universal way.

It seemed that the evolution of the discourses of our society since the last century have been ahead of psychoanalysis, but Lacan's formulations not only integrated this evolution but actually conceived it. It was waiting to be deciphered in its entirety so that the discoveries it involved could be understood. It anticipated certain aspects of the evolution of the modes of jouissance, often presenting them in the form of aphorisms whose equivocal or indecipherable meaning sometimes appeared 'conservative', whereas time has shown that the contrary was true.

For example, in the aphorism 'The woman does not exist', it was a case of showing that the article 'The' in 'the woman' – as the sexual law defined her as object of desire – could not be right, since it did not apply to all of her.[3] The status of object could not possibly describe the entire woman; the position of object could not possibly sum her up, because the woman as such is situated elsewhere, outside discourse. So that the signifier 'The woman' does not in fact exist in the symbolic order, and each woman has to reinvent the terms of her relation to the other.

As a statement, this has a tone that might appear 'patriarchal' in a caricatural way, whereas as an utterance it is in fact entirely feminist. We may wonder why someone would express something so entirely opposed to what they appeared to be saying. It is left as a question, but that is the style of the author, and so if we want to read him correctly, we have to decipher it using his explanations. It appears that this equivocation had a number of effects, since many readers took it at face value, whether they subscribed to it or not.

Psychoanalysis seemed to distance itself from the developments in society that were taking place in the 20th century – which were in part derived from psychoanalytic thinking itself – but within its ranks the Lacanian approach was already being worked out, and that is what ultimately allowed us to interpret its logics. They concern the way phallic jouissance defines not only masculinity but also the feminine, albeit differently, in the function of speech and the link to phallic objects of desire.[4]

Certain feminist discourses, which maintain that women's jouissance and subjectivity are completely equivalent to and symmetrical with those of men, thereby indicate their own jouissance at the level of the subject. There are others who point out that 'women's liberation' is not achieved through establishing a symmetry with the position of men, but rather through the deploying of woman's specificity, and they are referring to women's supplementary jouissance. So the two affirmations find their justification in different registers, because in all registers where it is a question of the performance and achievement of the speaking being, the feminine subject participates in phallic jouissance, whereas femininity as such is added to this following another logic within the framework of love life.

When phallic jouissance was considered to be exclusively masculine, femininity was supposed to be attainable only through the suppression or repression of infantile phallic jouissance actively deployed in the relation to the mother and in clitoral jouissance. Across civilisations, this imperative was applied in different ways, and nowadays some continue to do so through ritual mutilations, repressing all signs and realisations rooted in the jouissance of the subject of speech. During the last century, there was a massive shifting of the boundaries of the modes of jouissance. What was known as women's liberation consisted essentially in a widespread liberation of the function of woman as subject, of the phallic jouissance of the subject. In our societies, there is no longer any imperative to repress it in order to make way for a feminine jouissance, which can find its place at another subjective pole.

There is still, however, a confusion in the unconscious, in spite of the developments in discourse and ideology. For example, many little girls continue to think, when they develop a phallic jouissance in early childhood – through masturbation and the primary relation with the mother – that they have something masculine about them, and there is an imaginary guilt-laden borrowing from the attributes of other sex. Both the unconscious and contemporary discourse continue to create a radicalisation, in one direction, of feminine duality, while retaining a tendency towards the logic of the all-phallic, eliding the division into two poles, between what corresponds to a subject and what comes from being a woman. Maybe this is due in part to the fact that the imaginary and the mirror stage in childhood weigh so heavily, and lead to an imaginary model of phallic jouissance, while it is only later in life that the opening up of the subject occurs as a counterweight to this.

The two modes of sexuation that enable us to find a way through what we find in the contemporary world are both constituted on the basis of the phallic function, one in its entirety and the other only partially. They involve the phallic signifier, in the one case consisting in identifying with it, and in the other in desiring it. They deal both with the consequences of the Oedipus complex and with what is at stake in the real of the adult sexual encounter. They involve sexuated identification, as well as the choice of sexual object, including that of the same sex. These two logics of sexuation, therefore, cover a wide field of determination.

On the masculine side, phallic jouissance is at work in the form of phantasy, following the relation between the subject and his object a as part of himself; this schema conforms perfectly to the metaphor of Genesis. This relation of subject to their object according to phallic jouissance is just as valid for a female subject, so here we do see a symmetry reclaimed. On the specifically feminine side, there is also a jouissance of the phallus, desired and expected as such, and a jouissance of the Other as desire and as body, marked by the castration involved in the sexual relation.

The frontier between the masculine and the feminine is complex, and characterised by asymmetry. It is not simply a case of the phallus being on one side, and its absence on the other, because jouissance of the phallus is found on both sides. On the masculine side it is organised solely around the phallic function that creates the link of the phantasy between the subject and his object as a part of himself, while on the feminine side it is not the only mode of organisation. This new division that is still establishing itself in society in our time is what Lacan wrote on the blackboard in 1973, in the letters of his schema of the two logical modes of sexuation.[5] Initially people reacted with a certain stupor, and yet it proved to be nothing other than an expression of what was actually happening in Western societies at the time.

***

The logic of the masculine side, then, entirely obeys the phallic function, regulated by the subtraction of jouissance attributed to the Father, whether in the Oedipus complex or in the sexual relation. If he remains completely within this logic, the man oscillates between the position of the son deprived of jouissance and that of identification with the Father, from nothing to the all-phallic, in the register of having. A woman who remains within this logic oscillates between being the object of the Father's desire, or nothing.

The way sexuated identification and the object are determined is largely a matter of choice, even if it is an unconscious one. However, sexuated identification is one thing, and the choice of object is another, and it is quite possible and indeed common to make a heterosexual object choice while having adopted a sexuated identification with the other sex. The choice consists in either being entirely within the logic of the subject's phallic function, or in adding to it the part of feminine logic that is not totally derived from this, and the latter will involve a real subjective upheaval. The register of any of those attributes discovered by psychoanalysis and applied in its practice – the half, the not-all, the equivocal, the half-said – is infinitely more difficult to grasp and sustain than the register of the logic of the all or nothing, of extremes, of the 1 and the 0, which are operative in the majority of discourses and are derived exclusively from the phallic function. However, the not-all is closer to the real, and it can create a stability in the relation to the Other, and to the Other sex in particular. But still the discoveries made regarding anything that obeys a logic of the not-all are sometimes covered up and annulled by a radicalisation in terms of the all, invalidating such efforts and leading to their abandonment.

The logic of the 'all' does not correspond solely to traditional masculinity, but also to the whole spectrum of neurosis, which was long considered to be normal. Once Freud had argued that normal femininity resembled hysterical neurosis and normal masculinity, obsessional neurosis, Lacan's observations led us to establish something even more radical, enabling us to grasp the close relationship between all-phallic sexuation and neurosis. In neurosis, as in the masculine dimension, the same logic forms the basis of the castration of everyone through its agent who is the sole exception, the Father of the Oedipus complex or of the world of discourses. Where the phallic function alone prevails, as we have already emphasised, any subtraction of jouissance is carried forward onto the phantasy of an object as value of jouissance or exchange. This gives the subject the impression of refinding a completeness, since the complement is made from the part that was subtracted. This is how a logic of all or nothing is established, and is the wellspring of tragedy as well as comedy: you do not want anything if you cannot have everything, so will opt for nothing, since having it all is not in the realm of what is possible.

These extremes are both disturbing and rather hopeless, and are regularly found in neurosis and in the traditional traits of manliness. In this logic, love is separated from sexual jouissance. The woman whom the man cannot have jouissance of is the one who is loved; the man for whom the woman makes herself symbolically the object is loved, without having any regard for her own jouissance. This is the reason for the centrifugal nature of the masculine position, oscillating simultaneously or successively between the Other of love and the object of desire, introducing a mutually exclusive alternation where there is no need for one. Here we find the creation of a sort of third sex,[6] dividing the woman in two, the mother and the whore, realising on one side the son's castration and on the other the Father's potency.

The 'complementary' relation exclusively prescribed throughout the millennia by our sexual law, even though it varied widely, is a response to this logic grounded in neurosis. Like Genesis, it articulates the phantasy of a subject separated from his lost part, which is refound in some form or other, restoring him to completeness. With the current alterations in the model of the Father, certain aspects of neurosis are evolving, but still new forms of neurosis may lead back in different ways to a logic of the all and the exception.

***

The logic of the feminine side, then, does not entirely obey the phallic function of discourse. Within this framework the Father does not play the role of refusing castration while imposing it on everyone else; there is no exception who is responsible for the law of castration for everyone, with the result that the law is not necessarily applicable to everyone. This does not mean that a woman gives up entirely on the love of the Father, since we know how very present this is in feminine logics, for example for certain mystics. Lacan made them the model of a specifically feminine jouissance, but it is one where there is no sexuality. The love of the Father in this case is not comparable to that found in hysteria, where he continues to function as the exception. A 'sexual relation' in these terms can be constructed on the basis of two, whereas it cannot be so in terms derived from the phallic function, which has a place for only one jouissance within a sexual couple, and even that can hardly be called a jouissance.

The supplementary pathway offers a way out of neurosis, since it does without the function of the Father who is supposed to regulate jouissance but who in fact is the cause of neurosis. Its efficacy comes from a departure from phantasy, having a much closer connection with the real. While neurosis feeds a contradictory dependency on the function of the Father, actively supporting it while objecting to it in the unconscious, the logic of the not-all offers a way out. In this sense, the cure of neurosis in a certain register entails a development towards the logic of the not-all, which is not the prerogative of the feminine, but rather the logic of certain fundamental acts and discourses.

In this case, making oneself an object is added to desire, instead of being substituted for it; desire is added to the object. Ordinarily, the discourse of the law does not imply that the object should be active, but neither does it imply that it should be passive, and so it leaves the question in suspense. The woman's position cannot be reduced to lending herself to being the object, because her desire is also active in the construction of the sexual couple, and in other ways in her subjective realisations. The relation between partners in this case is not simply composed of 'one plus a', but consists of 'two ones plus a', two desires and two jouissances knotted together by the object that the woman makes of herself, so that the man's phallic jouissance and her own jouissance have this object in common. Access to a 'sexual relation' as such is now possible, as a relation between two desires knotted by the intermediary of a third term. It cannot be inscribed in a discourse, and can be constituted only in speech and in acts.

Feminine logic is a supplement to the phallic function of the law, representing a form of objection to it, whereas one might think that it actively confirms it. Actively making oneself the object does in reality constitute an objection to the law, which is derived from a logic in which the object, far from being active, has no speech. The terms articulated by this mode of jouissance, as is clearly shown in the Lacanian schema of sexuation,[7] deny the universality of the woman that is enshrined in law as if she were defined exclusively by the phallic function, and reduced to being the object of desire. This jouissance, however, is not for every woman, because not every woman wants to act, or is able to, according to this logic in an encounter. It is only valid within a specific couple, it cannot be written as a discourse, but has to be constantly rewritten. Love is not separated from desire, nor from jouissance. The man who has renounced the phallic function of the law and modified his phallic jouissance, is the one who is loved and desired by this specific woman. And the woman whose jouissance brings them together, the one he gives jouissance to and has jouissance of, is the one loved by the man, who has been given the latitude to deploy his phallic jouissance in a different way.

***

We can thus see how these two sexuated logics are contradictory, but they are only partially so. They are only contradictory if we remain within the order of the universal. Within the framework of a logic that allows for contradiction, different from traditional logic, they are not so. As long as we remain within the order of discourse and of universality, the position of each individual within the phallic function become symmetrical and can only become the source of discord. In order for an articulation of the two logics to be possible, we must recognise the fact that one of the logics approaches the other from a position of the universality of sexual law, while the other is partially outside it. Because one of the logics creates an obstacle to the 'sexual relation', the other aims to offer something supplementary to it, by adding another term in the imaginary and the real, where the symbolic has failed. When they come to be articulated together, it can only be outside the universal of discourse, and absolutely not in a way that is symmetrical and reciprocal between two terms.

The two sexuated logics do not create two different fields, with men lined up on one side and women on the other, because actually each individual positions themself on their unconsciously chosen side, even if the proportion of feminine logic remains much higher in women and the proportion of masculine logic higher in men. The difference does not consist in a symmetrical way in being in one or the other field, but rather in being either entirely within the phallic function and its phantasy, or in partially doing without it.

The sexuated identity that is constructed during childhood and beyond, through the choice made by the subject faced with what they encounter in the Other, is most often initially oriented according to the logic of the all. Even though the way our discourses and religions are evolving has tended to cause the prototype of the Name of the Father that they once promoted to disappear, the primary constructions of the unconscious, for every child and adolescent, willingly adopt the all-phallic that cuts instead of knots. Later on, a pathway may be followed, whether through psychoanalysis or some other way, that may tip a woman, or indeed a man, towards this other logic. Some men never manage to cross the threshold into another jouissance, and some will not even suspect its existence; others, at some point in their life, may position themselves in both the field of the phallic function and that of supplementary jouissance. This is the case for certain creatives and thinkers, because the activity of sublimation is closely correlated with this mode of jouissance. Some women may spend their entire lives within a masculine logic, derived solely from the phallic function, but many will find a way towards this other logic.

It is very difficult for the masculine logic of the all-phallic to form the basis of a 'sexual relation', in the sense of knotting two jouissances together, because it is entirely caught up in the function that opposes this. Because it sets up a subject driven towards the object[8] that is the equivalent of a part that has been subtracted from him, and it consists in 'having jouissance of' rather than 'having jouissance'; this is omnipresent in discourse, giving primacy to the relation of having over that of being. Within this schema, the sexual act makes a body into the metaphor of the jouissance of the other body, so that the other jouissance remains excluded. Desire is ceaselessly renewed, through the carrying forward of the portion of jouissance that has been subtracted onto an object, thus negating the subtraction.[9] This 'complementary' way of relating surely remains the reference for the greatest number of love relations, but it does not form the relation that it is believed to be possible to attain. This is because it is not a question of complementarity of one with the other, but rather of the subject with himself, and fundamentally it includes only one subject within the autoerotism of phallic jouissance.

When it is the sole mode of relation, and when there is no supplementary relation based upon it, this 'complementary' mode may give rise to jouissance of the master-slave type, along the lines of a masochistic contract, whether voluntary or not. It may also give rise to incessant phallic discord, or even to depression. The woman's function as phallic object is strongly represented when she is primarily the wife or partner, the daughter or the lover of another man. The man who ceases to desire his partner the moment the act has been carried out, the moment she has 'yielded', or very shortly afterwards, is one who has no defence against the castration he is subject to in the sexual act, except through the carrying forward of the subtracted jouissance onto another object. He eludes it and annuls it, and then carries it forward intact. This mode of surplus jouissance aims at a subjective position that is always orientated by the phallic function of the phantasy, ensuring that none of the other jouissance, the supplement of femininity, should intrude. Hence the cataloguing of women along the lines of 'he will have had jouissance of her', rather than 'he will have made her have jouissance'.

Nowadays this kind of 'complementary' relation may be initiated and pursued by a woman, strictly within the framework of the phallic function of discourse being imposed on the partner in an inverted form, or else by carrying forward the subtraction of jouissance encountered in each relation onto other partners. A number of discourses in the media vie with one another in making much of the fact that some women appear to achieve this kind of symmetry of jouissance in a masculine way. The women who, at least for a part of their lives, participate in this inversion in the form of mirroring, while holding on to a phallic jouissance, encounter the same castration and the same failure of the 'sexual relation' within this framework. By carrying forward onto another the value of what has been subtracted from them in each act, they also revert to and perpetuate the annulling of the absence of the two, without offering any supplement to it. Certain militant feminist and homosexual movements have developed their discourses along the lines of this mirrored phallic logic. This can only lead to a profound misunderstanding in the future of the relations between man and woman, but perhaps it has been necessary to pass through this stage in order to achieve a degree of political and historical progress.

Some men may also participate only partially in the phallic function, if their aim is to give jouissance to a woman and to respond to her desire rather than having jouissance of her. The possible double meaning of the jouissance of the woman – whether she has jouissance, in the imaginary register of the phallus, or whether one has jouissance of her in the register of the signifier – is always potentially operative in the sexual relation, but one of these generally takes precedence over the other.

The meaning and the mode of orgasm are different in the two cases. In the case where 'causing jouissance' prevails, the man shares in feminine jouissance, and is hardly any more preoccupied than the woman is with the mythical Father or God who is supposed to subtract phallic jouissance and elide that of the woman. In this case, the woman's jouissance and her orgasm are essential and necessary, and trigger his own. In the case where 'having jouissance of' prevails, the man has only the phallus and the Father who is in command of it as his partner. The woman's jouissance remains elided, and her orgasm is not necessary and may even be unwelcome.

No one emerges from a sexual act quite the same as they were before it. Annulling and repressing the gap between the two jouissances leaves each individual exiled from jouissance. Recognising the gap and constructing a suppleance that allows a knotting of the jouissances has other consequences. Maybe this is the reason why the phenomenology of the sexual act is sometimes described according to an inverse curve for each sex. The classic description of a sexual approach demanded, or instigated, from the masculine side, comes with the adage *post coitum omne animal triste*.[10] Whereas a prudent, even anxious approach from the feminine side is often described as being followed by a state of serenity. Of course, these classic profiles are only types among many others, and in any case have been considerably altered by contemporary social developments. So we see today many women having multiple relations in a purely phallic way, carrying forward the castration of the sexual act from one partner to the next, and participating entirely in the masculine logic of the all-phallic. Whereas some men, in sex, adopt the inhibition or the passivity that were formerly the lot of women according to the sexual law, or else they may actively share in the supplementary jouissance of a woman.

II. Knotting through supplementary jouissance

The fact that masculine and feminine jouissances are partially in contradiction to one another does not mean that they cannot be linked. The absence of the sexual relation, in the Lacanian sense, as the absence of a relation that can be written between two sexes, does not mean that it is impossible as such, but just that it is impossible to inscribe in the universe of discourse. At least this is the case where the current state of discourse is concerned, the legacy of an eroded Christianity, and its institutions have not yet totally redistributed the sexes' functions, now that the Father of all of us, the Name of the Father, is no longer universally called upon to hold them together. Because such a relation cannot be written in a universal way, this has left each individual, each couple, the responsibility and the latitude to choose a number of small pathways to work one out, outside discourse. This shows that the possibility of such a relation does exist, while still not constituting a model for others, because it can only be constructed between two people, in a real experience, according to whether the unconscious of the one and the other manage to achieve some kind of knotting together at specific points.

The phallic function, that of the subject completed by his phallic object, may thus play a part in the knotting of two jouissances, whereas it constitutes an obstacle if it operates alone in the process. In the former case, it partially departs from the phantasy that contains it. This may be difficult to grasp, but it is essential to our argument. Since the phallic function operates between a jouissance and its castration, followed by a surplus jouissance that has to be recuperated, in order for it to be possible for a knotting to take place with the other's mode of jouissance, it is necessary for the phallic function to disappear at a certain point. Given that the man, according to this logic, encounters a partner who is nothing other than his imaginary phallic complement, he has to give up on this mode of the phallus within this framework, in order for his jouissance not to be solely autoerotic, so that he should not be 'cheated, encountering nothing but his bodily complement'.[11] A man may have access to a relation of two jouissances by accepting this form of castration[12] involving the organising phallic signifier of the sexual law, consisting in 'having jouissance of'. He has to accept the loss of the phallic feminine object promised to him by the law, to make room for another jouissance, which in return will endow him with another sort of phallus. On this condition, his phallic jouissance can be articulated with the other jouissance of the woman.

The sexual law means that the man aims at the lack in the woman that in fact concerns only him, where the partner has to be castrated in order to cause his desire. Since this no longer has the force of law, he has had to mourn the loss of the castration formerly sought out in the woman, and in so doing has discovered that the real lack in the woman is something quite different, and consists in depending on his own desire in order to have access to her own jouissance. Indeed, if her own jouissance is to make herself into the object she offers to the man, and in return she can have jouissance of the phallus that she endows him with and that he gives to her in this way, the whole process can only be set in motion on the basis of the desire of the man when he participates in it. Beyond this see-sawing, when the man rediscovers the phallus he has been deprived of in an imaginary form, he no longer receives it from a Father from whom he had stolen it, but from the jouissance of this particular woman.

The original equation is based on the formula of his having the phallus in the name of the Father; this shifts when a particular woman has given herself to him, and he has made her have jouissance, so he 'has' her in a quite different way. It is no longer a question of the phallus that is at stake in the phallic function of the law, and it is no longer a case of the process which, on the basis of the phallic subtraction from the sexual relation, produces the signifier aimed at having jouissance of the feminine object as his bodily complement. It is now a question of the phallus as symbol of feminine jouissance in the sense that it arouses the latter. This modality of the phallus is at play in all kinds of achievements, and may at times lead us to suspect that a woman's jouissance may lie behind a man's success.

We may indeed think that access to this kind of relation has been facilitated today, now that the incidence of the sexual law which was once universal has been significantly reduced and is only locally enforced. This is probably true, even though it cannot be measured, and people say that there is a vast reinvention of love today, which involves a linking of two jouissances, to construct, step by step, what is called a couple. It is part of what has taken the place of the traditional relation of man and woman, based on the 'elementary structures of kinship', towards that which is now largely rooted in the sexual couple: the multiple ways in which the sexual relation creates the social bond. Beyond marriage and its laws, what is active nowadays is the sexual encounter outside the law, and the random and ephemeral composition of the bonds that it may form.

The sexual encounter is a new type of bond resulting from the contingencies of chance, and is a source of a possible femininity that deploys its other logic, because there is no such thing as femininity in itself, no more so than there is a masculine position as such that could be linked to it. Such bonds result from encounters and the process at play that knots together a relation from them. When a man gives up the phallic function of the law of the Father, he submits himself to a form of castration for the particular woman, while she makes herself into the object for him and has jouissance from this. One term falls away where the phallic function is concerned, while another is formed in the jouissance that unites the couple. Initially the man is deprived of the object as complement, since the woman is no longer reduced to that, but then he finds another, conferred on him by the woman's jouissance. He is castrated of his complement from the perspective of the law, but finds a supplement that is specific to him. The realisation of an actual 'sexual relation' goes through a preparatory stage of reduction in the initial units that will be put together, and this is why the metaphor of meiosis is quite appropriate. The woman's jouissance, which is not inscribed in discourse, remains silent, like an absence,[13] but it certainly does exist, and is just as real as speech that acts. She satisfies the phallic function through making herself into the object that she represents within it, but she adds the supplement that she creates in her own way.

The female orgasm is often present in this supplementary jouissance, but it is not a necessary or a specific part of it. Vocalisation is not proportional to the intensity of the orgasm, but on the contrary, the orgasm in itself provokes a rattle, a panting, rather than a cry as such. A cry may be the manifestation of a defence against a feeling of invasion, against the abandonment to jouissance, rather than of a feminine jouissance as such. In this way it certainly has as its corollary the mythical Father. In feminine jouissance, whether accompanied by orgasm or not, it is not a question of a phantasy that causes the Father or one of his manifestations to appear; jouissance is not aroused by an all-powerful Other, but by an Other who has revealed his flaw, while being decisive in his desire.

In this mode of relation, the man's phallic jouissance no longer refers to the Father, is not regulated by his function, and is no longer subject to his castration. It is deployed in a way that, through aiming at the object, the man encounters the other, whereas the woman, aiming at the other, encounters an absence. This is the point where the man believes he desires the woman; when he encounters the Other, he loves her, while the woman believes she loves the Other in the man, and when she encounters an absence, she desires him.[14] The man's jouissance, stretched between the object and the Other, finds this to be a more satisfactory solution. It is now possible for a relation to be knotted between the object the woman makes of herself, her jouissance, which creates it and offers it, and the man's phallic jouissance. In this case, the woman is both the Other and the object, and the man can relate to each of these two terms in one being, instead of splitting the relation to the mother on the one hand and to the whore on the other, in a centrifugal way.

The 20th century offered a number of famous examples of this way of knotting a 'sexual relation', for instance among the surrealists, where enacted feminine desire was very clear and caused men, at the price of giving up on a previous position, to deploy creative capacities on a vast scale. This discovery gave rise to enthusiastic slogans such as 'the woman is the future of the man'. Although no longer idealised in the same way, this type of relation is part of contemporary life, and has in fact become the default position in love relations, even if it remains difficult to actually achieve. Where it can be, it represents a perennial modality for the sexual couple, a durable relation that can function without being time limited.[15]

An actual 'sexual relation' between two jouissances can, then, be achieved, but not in the way of a complementary relation in terms of 'one plus a'. It requires a supplement and involves the woman's ensuring that her own desire is included, herself creating the object she makes of herself, knotting together three terms: 'one plus one, plus a'. We can speak here of the 'sexual relation' in the sense that it now concerns two sexes and not one sex and its object and also, in the Freudian sense, it can unite the affectionate and sensual currents aiming at the same person. It is formed as an exception, not, however, in the sense of being exceptional and rare, but in the sense of being a partial exception from what has been established by discourse and the law according to the phallic function.

This exception is no more universal than is that of the Father, but it is unary in so far as it is valid only for one unit. This type of relation does not form the basis for any rule, and cannot be written in any discourse, because only the part of the relation that satisfies the phallic function of the law can be written in it. The supplementary jouissance that establishes it is an utterance that subverts the function of the Father, the phallic function, as well as the sexuated identifications promulgated by the law, since it redistributes the burden of the real castration entailed in the sexual act between the two partners. Rather than castration being unilaterally on the feminine side, as decreed by the sexual law, it is now shared by each partner in a different way. This is the sense in which it allows there to be a 'sexual relation'.

In our Western societies today, unions between couples are often ephemeral; separation and divorce have almost become the norm, and it has become ordinary and acceptable for a single human life to involve being part of a succession of couples. This particular way of relating involves a complex process, but it is certainly real, and often lasting. The process is obviously not the same as the one involved in the formation of couples limited by time. Indeed, the mode of relation that is created by a woman's supplementary jouissance has no time limit, thanks to its own logic, while the other modalities of forming couples do have a time limit. Once the signifying institutions of the Name of the Father and the sexual law no longer impose the indissolubility of marriage, there is no symbolic third term to guarantee that the couple will stay together if they were united solely on the contingent basis of love. Supplementary jouissance and the relation it creates do not involve a temporal limit.

It is hard to say whether this way of relating has developed significantly and become far more widespread than it was in the past. But even though it is assuredly the most real part of the 'sexual relation' there is still no way of writing it in discourse. As psychoanalysis has shown, this type of relation is favoured by the fact that a number of men, more often than in the past, decline to identify with the mythical Father who forms the basis of the sexual law, 'who has jouissance of all the women', to the extent that they have discovered that this function bars their access to the other sex as such. For a long time it was thought, both in psychoanalysis and elsewhere, that a satisfactory realisation of masculinity consisted in identifying with the Father, whereas current developments show that such an identification consists only in having jouissance autoerotically, even within a sexual relation, and eliding the Other in the female partner. Just like the phallic function that supports it, it is an obstacle to the 'sexual relation' as such, a relation of two. On a wider scale, it appears that feminine jouissance opens up a pathway to another jouissance for the man, without constituting a barrier to his phallic jouissance.

Nevertheless, there are a number of persistent difficulties in achieving this type of relation. The man will often recoil when faced with something he might find anxiety-provoking in this 'castration', even though it could facilitate a more effective relation. Confronted with what is demanded by the jouissance of the other and with whatever forms an obstacle to his own, some make the choice of dodging the whole issue. Similarly, it is not easy to give up on the feminine 'castration' that is so sought after by masculine desire, even though it has become more apparent to him that the woman's lack does not reside there, but rather in her dependence on his desire. On the other hand, a number of men now situate their own jouissance in whatever it takes to make a woman have jouissance, and not merely to have jouissance of her, for some even to the extent of becoming estranged from their own jouissance.

Women are today less prepared to accept the position of object of desire, because it is now widely accepted that in order to have access to this liberated jouissance, it is necessary to reject the idea of being an object. This mistake does not consist in preaching a feminine jouissance as such, but rather a phallic jouissance that mirrors that of the man. In fact, there is no need to reject the position of object of the man's phantasy in order to have access to feminine jouissance, but there is good reason not to identify with it, because that is something entirely different. It is precisely because is has become abundantly clear that a woman cannot be reduced to a position as object, and that there is a gentler way of paying her debt to the phallic function in order to have access to her own jouissance.

A number of women have adopted the masculine logic of the all-phallic – whether on a provisional basis or not – in all domains, sexual as well as professional. They also participate in the 'debasement of sexual life' that Freud described in men, choosing a despised object in order to have jouissance of him, while the man who is loved is not desired. This mirroring leads back to a separation of love and sex as is classically described to be the case for men.[16] The insistence on a jouissance without love may appear centre stage here, when it is confused with having access to feminine jouissance. It is as if it were easier for the unconscious to tip back into the all-phallic rather than trying to articulate two jouissances and being in the realm of the half-said, subscribing to a discourse but capable of articulating itself outside of this. Conversely, a number of men have an inhibited and anxious attitude to sex, especially when they are confronted with excessive phallic jouissance in the other sex.

***

Each individual enters the field of the sexual act according to their sexuated identification, determined on the basis of the sexual law that distributes phallic having and being between the sexes, whether or not they accept it, refuse it, or deal with it in other ways. Even though the law no longer has the force of law, the 'sexual relation' is still determined by something that has nothing to do with sexuality: being and having. In love relations, each individual finds themself caught up in the desire to make One that hovers over the sexual act; this refers unconsciously to the maternal pole, the imaginary source of what consists in making one of two, each one presenting themself as the object of a jouissance that was previously banned and forbidden. Incest haunts the sexual act as a return of the repressed, not only because through its exclusions it forms the basis of the symbolic order for everyone, but also because the universal lack of union of jouissances calls for an original mythical union which, unlike the other one, will not fail.

Supplementary jouissance makes up for the lack of the One by achieving a union of two through the intermediary of a third term, and not by making the One out of two, which is no more possible with the sexual partner than it was with the mother. This jouissance, by maintaining the object it creates of itself as a third term, allows the two jouissances of the sexual couple to be knotted together indirectly.[17] While it is not possible to create a 'sexual relation' in this sense on the basis of the phallic function alone, it is not possible to create one without it either. The object as third term is so essential to the process of knotting the jouissances of the two partners that, if it is not created by a woman who also takes up its position, it is often replaced by something entirely different. An ideal, a child, or even a symptom is what holds together so many couples, as has been widely observed both within and outside psychoanalysis. In such cases it is not always a case of the object as third term of a supplementary jouissance, but rather the object linking two phallic jouissances.

The articulation of two jouissances in the supplementary relation does not mean that of the two subjects, even if two desires are involved. The subject in this is certainly the position of the man, and the object is certainly the position of the woman, but in this case the object is active. The passivity that is usually attributed to the object now, on the contrary, changes into a certain activity. While phallic jouissance proceeds via displacement – carrying forward, metonymy – supplementary jouissance proceeds above all via metaphor, through substitution of the one who loves for the one who is loved, of the one who has jouissance for the one of whom one has jouissance.

Confronted with the lack of conjunction of jouissances radicalised by the castrating function of the Father and sexual law, feminine love and its mode of jouissance keep emerging in a constant attempt to reduce this gap. This supplementary relation is articulated in the imaginary and the real, but not in the symbolic of discourse, since it does not belong there. It is a fact of speech in action, not of a statement in discourse; it is in contradiction with the law, which states inscribes itself, and is articulated in something that is half-said (*mi-dit*), an equivocation.

The phallic dialectic does not allow for the knotting of two terms, but only the phantasy of a constantly flowing 'flux' between plus and minus, whereas the supplementary relation involving supplementary jouissance adds something that allows for a knotting of three. The sharing of castration between the two sexes allows for a relation between two jouissances, but this is not done by the law of discourse which places it unilaterally on the feminine side. For this to occur, the terms of castration that operate within discourse need to move outside of it, in the imaginary and the real, and inversely, and this allows the knot to be tied. The partner who lacks the phallus in one dimension has it in another, and vice versa.

Feminine jouissance, with the love that it usually includes, thus makes up for the absence of the 'sexual relation' by elaborating the necessary imaginary and real conditions to construct the particular relation between a particular couple, beyond what is allowed in discourse. It constantly circulates around the lack, around the hole in jouissance, each time bringing an equivalent but still new response to it. By repeating the relation that entails this lack of jouissance, the increasingly precise approach of the suppleance gradually reduces the gap. In this case, the object is not to be found elsewhere through a carrying forward of the subtracted jouissance, but is worked through *in situ* on the basis of what is lacking. It does not mask the lack of 'sexual relation', but creates one to make up for it. It confers the symbol of the phallus on the man in quite another way than the universal attribute stemming from the phallic function in the name of the Father.

For the man now, love is no longer separate from sexual jouissance. There are many literary testimonies showing how this form of castration, in the relation of a man with a woman, opens up the pathway to another jouissance, while still leaving space for a fertile phallic jouissance.

III. Feminine jouissance and the social bond

By definition, supplementary jouissance is absent from discourse, since it creeps in silently, and does not do what discourse expects. This means that it leaves very few traces, but does have powerful effects in sexuality, in the social relation between the sexes, and elsewhere. This jouissance shared between the partners of the two sexes has made the absence of the sexual relation less obvious. In this way, two stages of the relation between the sexes are determined: that of the social law and its jurisdiction, and that of the real of intimacy that is not part of this, since it allows something to occur in silence that is elided by the law. The fact that it functions in the un-said and the half-said involves a recognition of the flaw in the 'sexual relation' and a permanent working-out of what can make up for it.

There is a comparable logic in artistic sublimation, which aims to make up not only for the absence of the 'sexual relation', but also for the fundamental lack of jouissance, which is hollowed out by the prohibition of incest. Psychoanalysis has developed these ideas, because Freud, using the terms that were current in his time, proposed that feminine desire was seldom directed towards creative sublimation – and this was certainly true at the time, since it was forbidden by law. On the other hand, in the second half of the 20th century, Lacan showed how close the process of sublimation is to that of the supplementary jouissance of the woman, even when it happens to be the sublimation of a man. In this case and many others, Lacan's psychoanalytic thinking took things up where Freud had left them, i.e. in the discourse of the phallic function, which the sexual law prescribed in a way that was still virtually universal. He took it still further, showing what can be worked out beyond that function and that law, which has become more obvious since they no longer exclusively prescribe their specific way of relating within our societies.

Sublimation does not annul the lack inherent in jouissance, any more than does feminine logic, but it does supplement it in a similar way, by elaborating the imaginary conditions necessary to refind a form of forbidden jouissance, but without transgression. And similarly, sublimation needs time to circulate around the lack, over and over again, to repeat and adjust a response, which is constantly renewed while still being structurally equivalent, with the aim of reducing the gap. In this sense, there is no temporal limit on either sublimation or feminine supplementary jouissance at the horizon of their logic, apart from death. Nor do they consist in substituting themselves for sexual jouissance, as is far too often thought, but rather they operate alongside it.

In Lacan's anthropological approach to Edgar Allan Poe's 'Purloined Letter',[18] he described in a metaphorical way how the two modes of jouissance of the sexes had evolved in contemporary society. When he took it up again in 1971, he stressed that the possession of the letter, which the minister stole as a phallic instrument of power over the Queen, did not lead him to what one might have expected in terms of manhood. On the other hand, when the letter was taken away from him by Dupin, far from considering that he would collapse in the face of ridicule when he discovered that he no longer had the letter, Lacan proposed that he would have had his function as a man restored to him by this very castration. The Queen would no longer 'contest the potency she has . . . disarmed him of', and the minister's power 'will be affirmed in proportion to the masochism that had shadowed him'.[19]

In this commentary, we can discern Lacan's position regarding the development of the relation of man and woman at this specific moment in time, towards the end of the last century when our society was undergoing such extraordinary upheavals. He commented on the text as a metaphor of what had taken place in the relation of the sexes, considering that Man, at that point in History, had been deprived of the signifying phallus, which he had wrongfully seized, just like the minister who had the letter taken from him that he had stolen from the Queen. Lacan proposed that he would not suffer from this in his functioning as a man, because, on the contrary, this castration liberated him from the 'feminisation' he had undergone as a punishment for purloining this sign which actually belongs to the woman, and which is something quite different from having the symbol via the pathway of making her have jouissance.

Throughout the history of civilisations, myths, religions and traditions, we can trace the fact that the symbol of what consists in making a woman have jouissance becomes conflated with the signifier of what the man has in the name of the Father in order to have jouissance of the woman, amalgamating it with the penis. The inversion that occurs from one to the other in these symbolic systems is striking. The phallus, instead of being a principle of sexual jouissance shared by the two sexes, becomes the principle of usufructuary jouissance of one sex by the other.

Instead of being a symbol of victory over castration, which would allow the conjunction of their jouissances, the signifying phallus becomes the principle of the unilateralisation of castration on the side of the woman and of the jouissance to be had of her. Instead of attempting to join two jouissances together, it only concerns one of them, and so retreats even further from jouissance. From having been the symbol of the jouissance of a woman, in the subjective genitive sense, the phallus has become the signifier of the jouissance of the woman, objective genitive, in the sense that one has jouissance of her, in the name of the Father and then of the Man.

We regularly find there is a misalignment between what a civilisation inscribes and represents regarding a 'sexual relation' in its myths, and how it occurs in practice in the real social bonds established between the sexes. The civilisations that aimed to symbolise what it was that caused a woman to have jouissance, such as the wisdom of Eastern Antiquity, were quite able concurrently to oppress women's jouissance. Furthermore, they developed the system of polygamy, which consists in denying the castration of the sexual act by demonstrating that the man can have jouissance of several women, or an even larger number, as the harem was supposed to show.

The contemporary deconstruction of the signifier of the Name of the Father, and of the signifying phallus linked to it, finds its metaphor in the outcome of the Purloined Letter. The Western world has, in sum, taken the letter back from the Man it created, which gave him the right, or even the duty, to have jouissance of the other sex. Lacan's 1969 commentary went as far as suggesting that a man, just like the minister, does not become ridiculous just because he no longer has it. The castration of an unwarranted signifier restores him to his function as a man, which is not to attribute it to himself, but to conquer the sign or the symbol by sharing the jouissance it causes with a woman.

When Lacan made the surprising observation that the minister is feminised when he seizes the sign of feminine jouissance, out of which he makes an instrument of his power over her, it presupposes his notion of what characterises manhood as such. He situates masculinity as being what consists in conquering the sign by arousing the woman's jouissance, and not in the possession of the universal signifier in the name of a Father who aims to curtail his jouissance, which feminises the man in the eyes of the Father. This is certainly a remarkable interpretation of one of the well-springs of the relation between the sexes, which he pursued throughout his commentary on Poe's tale, over a number of years, and which removes any equivocation, if indeed there still were any, on the position he maintained and the way he deciphered the relation between the sexes.

A possible articulation of masculine and feminine jouissances takes place via a logic that is not derived solely from the phallic function. It never consists in returning to the law, but in going a step further. Freud observed the extent to which the repression necessary for clitoral jouissance caused neurosis in women. That is no longer the case. A certain form of the logic of the all-phallic has disappeared, or has been redistributed. Lacan's work proposed that the man needed to give up the all-phallic, if he wanted to share the half-said of the other jouissance, and this is broadly what is happening nowadays on a vast scale.

The new logic that he described and worked out to account for what was happening in terms of the specific mode of a woman's jouissance is also the logic of practising analysts, in relation to their position and their discourse. This is not to say that the practice of psychoanalysis is especially feminine, of course, and indeed the entire history of the field argues against that, but it works on the basis of the logic that is called the 'not-all', because is it not derived solely from the phallic function of discourse.

This observation makes us reformulate the characteristics of the 'sexual relation' between man and woman in our century. We can see that in order for there to be any chance of an actual relation, which can only be decided two by two, it is not a question of rejecting the sexual law and its grammar of the masculine subject coupled with his object, but rather of grasping the fact that it is not the whole story about the articulation of desires and jouissances between them. Because once the phallic function is no longer a universal law imposed as such, it still remains the pathway to such a relation, so long as it is now clear that it does not suffice on its own. At a time when the vast majority of Western women, and progressively others, too, are developing lives as free subjects with their own means and their own achievements, a number of them persist in imagining the man they desire in a way prescribed by the law, in the same way as the phallic function remains a powerful mode of desire for a number of men. In our time, then, the challenge has been to apply a new logic – which does not proceed from the traditional logic of the 'all' and of non-contradiction – to the relation between man and woman, as well as in other areas. It organises contradictory terms as different poles which not only do not negate one other, but also actually contribute to constructing and inscribing a knotting between them.

Although Freud stressed that the unconscious did not recognise contradiction, and although Lacan, responding to Freud's logic, took the decision to invent a new one, we have to accept that the unconscious still has a tendency towards the all-phallic. All its fundamental metaphors, as we can decipher them according to the likely ways in which they were originally constructed, derive from a law that prescribes refinding a whole while blocking the actual joining of the two sexes. The various moments in history when the founding metaphors of monotheism spread and won over the populations of various continents involved a violent eradication of any terms that were, or seemed to be, contradictory.[20] Any progress humanity has made in terms of the advance of knowledge since then has occurred during times of the ebbing away and abandonment of such metaphors of the All. The unconscious works to construct logics of the All. And other logics regularly spring up here when these latter show their fault lines and impasses.

Nowadays, when the relation between man and woman inscribed within the institutions of marriage has shown itself to be failing, the cards have been reshuffled, and the logics of the not-all are being deployed. Psychoanalysis could be considered to be the very essence of the laboratory of a logic of the not-all, and especially its Lacanian field, which is an extension of the Freudian field. An analysis consists in approaching and deconstructing the fundamental metaphors of the unconscious, and not in consolidating them, as many psychoanalysts believed for a long time.

Modernity has realised that the system of the Name of the Father emerged from a cut between the sexes, supported by the obstacle to the sexual relation that is phallic jouissance, leading to a hierarchical articulation between them of the 1 and the object. Opening up a pathway to get around this, and learning nevertheless to still use it, produces a redistribution of the functions at stake. The consequences are not that the woman is no longer the object of desire, but rather that she only lends herself to being the object according to her own desire, and that changes everything.

A psychoanalysis does not, as was thought for many years, effect a correct implementation of the metaphor of the prototype of the Father, but works towards smoothing out the costly and painful way in which neurosis implements it during childhood in our time. It aims to substitute modes of knotting that are created on a case-by-case basis, and to facilitate the necessary functions of the father albeit in different ways, leaving space for another logic. And hence it can lead to a subjective position based on relating to the other sex or with sex in general from a position of 'not-all, in a certain number of cases, which will grow significantly as psychoanalysis becomes capable of tackling this challenge on a larger scale.

IV. Jouissance and orgasm

The set of phallic significations linked to the function of the Father is in the process of shrinking, along with the belief system that underpinned it, while the phallic jouissance of the subject who does not depend on it is more and more present. Likewise, the symbol of the phallus which in its imaginary form is based on feminine jouissance never ceases to confirm its determining function, while the signifying system that aims at 'having jouissance of' the woman no longer predominates.

Where feminine jouissance is concerned, however, we can observe a paradoxical effect as religious prohibition has been lifted as a result of the weakening of belief, and when sexological experiments on the sexual relation published their results on the female orgasm. Lacan commented on this subject in the 1960s, when many women became depressed because they could not have an orgasm during sex, whereas they had not been before. It was at that time that he laid down the foundations of his elaboration of feminine jouissance, emphasising that it had been defined by psychoanalysis on the basis of a subjective position, rather than by orgasm. The distinction was important, because the emphasis that was placed on orgasm by the sexological discourses in their definition of jouissance is not, as such, a criterion of jouissance in the psychoanalytic sense. It is defined subjectively even though it is a bodily phenomenon, and there may be jouissance whether or not it involves orgasm.

For example, Lacan could say that 'I don't see why I would exclude sexual conjunction from the dimension of jouissance, which seems to be a dimension which is absolutely coextensive with the body. But that this should be orgasm does not seem to be necessary'.[21] The woman's orgasm may take place within the framework of a supplementary jouissance, specific to femininity, but it occurs more often within the framework of phallic jouissance during the sexual relation or masturbation. So defining jouissance by the presence of orgasm is correct only in the ordinary or sexological sense, but is not so in our field.[22]

Making a woman's orgasm a necessary criterion of feminine jouissance often consists in conflating the latter with phallic jouissance, which more easily leads to orgasm than supplementary jouissance does. However, a woman may also believe that the most important thing for her is to achieve orgasm, regardless of whether it happens within the subjective framework of a phallic jouissance or a truly feminine jouissance. This is a point of view that cannot be argued with, because orgasm is a bodily response that is essential to the maintenance of the subject, and is often considered to be a vital necessity, however it may be achieved in practice.

Psychoanalysis by definition encourages whatever sustains the subject without the need to pay the price with an unbearable symptom. But nevertheless, when we speak of feminine jouissance and phallic jouissance in psychoanalysis, we need to define them clearly and distinguish them from one another. Women who hold on to phallic jouissance may experience orgasm more frequently, but their jouissance is characterised by autoerotism, and does not allow them easy access to love or to having jouissance of the other as body. The same goes for the man, and if he can share in supplementary jouissance, the woman's will arouse his own, and the dimension of love can then be present.

Notes

1 See Gisèle Chaboudez, 'Semblances et différences, de l'hystérie à la fémninité', *Figures de la psychanalyse*, No. 27, 'L'hystérie', Toulouse, Érès, 2014.
2 Notably in Gayle Rubin, 'The Traffic in Women: Notes on the "Political Economy" of Sex', *Towards an Anthropology of Women*, ed. Ranya Reiter, New York, Monthly Review Press, 1975; Judith Butler, *Gender Trouble*, New York, Routledge, 1990.
3 This notion is commented on earlier, taken from the seminar *D'un discours qui ne serait pas du semblant*, op. cit., pp. 107–8.
4 On this point, see also my 'Semblances et différences, de l'hystérie à la féminité', op. cit.
5 Lacan, *Encore*, op. cit., p. 78.
6 Lacan's expression to designate the two feminine modalities that had already been described by Freud; see *La topologie et le temps*, seminar of 9 January 1979.
7 See Lacan, *Encore*, op. cit., p. 78.
8 We can see this clearly in Lacan's schema, referred to earlier, on p. 78 of *Encore*, ibid. On the side of the masculine logic of the all-phallic, a subject is in a relation to an object *a* in the feminine field, with the phallic signifier as his reference, without his having jouissance of it.
9 The carrying forward onto another feminine object, and especially onto another man's woman, the moment the sexual act is completed, is what characterises the myth of Don Juan, which brings together two ways of re-phallicising the man whom the sexual relation de-phallicises. It represents the dream of a man who would not lose the phallus in the encounter with feminine jouissance, and it is linked to the position of identification with the Father who has jouissance of all the women, and so of other men's women.
10 To which Lacan added that we should not forget the rest of the sentence: '*praeter mulierum gallum que*' – 'apart from women and cocks'. Jacques Lacan, *L'objet de la psychanalyse,* seminar of 27 April 1966.
11 Jacques Lacan, *Logic of the Phantasy*, seminar of 31 May 1967.
12 As Lacan described it: 'there is no chance for a man to have jouissance of a woman's body, in other words, to make love, without castration, that is, something that says no to the phallic function'. Lacan, *Encore*, op. cit., pp. 71–2, translation modified.
13 See Lacan, '. . . *Or Worse* ', op. cit., p. 104.
14 This kind of intersection is explored in Jacques Lacan, *L'acte psychanalytique*, seminar of 27 March 1968.
15 What certain current proclamations about the 'end of the couple' misunderstand (see Marcela Iacub, 'La Fin du couple', Paris, Stock, 2016).
16 On this point, see my 'Partition du sexe et de l'amour', *Figures de la psychanalyse*, No. 23, Toulouse, Érès, 2012.
17 This way of knotting, referred to earlier, is mentioned by Lacan in *Les Non-dupes Errent*, seminar of 15 January 1974.

18 See Jacques Lacan, 'The seminar on the Purloined Letter', *Écrits*, op. cit., pp. 6–48, and also *D'un discours qui ne serait pas du semblant*, op. cit., pp. 92–8.

19 Jacques Lacan, Preface to the *Points* edition of the *Écrits*, Paris, Seuil, 1970, p. 8.

20 On this point, the work of Jan Assman is crucial; see his *Moses the Egyptian*, Cambridge, Harvard University Press, 1997; *Of God and Gods*, University of Wisconsin Press, 2008; and *The Price of Monotheism*, Stanford University Press, 2009.

21 Just before this, he also said that, 'No one has yet definitively proven that woman has to have an orgasm to fulfil her role as woman. And the proof is that everyone is still debating what this is, the famous female orgasm. Nevertheless, this metaphysics has taken on such a weight, I know a lot of women who have become ill in not being sure that they are really experiencing enjoyment, when in fact they are not that unhappy with what they have, and if they hadn't been told that it wasn't that, they wouldn't be so preoccupied with it'. *The Object of Psychoanalysis*, seminar of 27 April 1966.

22 Lacan had noted, as mentioned earlier, that the female orgasm is relatively rare in the animal kingdom, but since it is sometimes observed, it shows that its existence is possible, and that in any case the frequency of extended copulations pointed to a jouissance different from orgasm.

Chapter 7

Redistribution of jouissances

I. Extension of the field of phallic jouissance

In our civilisation today, phallic jouissance is recognised explicitly as being something that belongs to women as well as men, in so far as is it a jouissance of the subject and not of a sex. Women who develop their functioning as subjects through their achievements, performance and professions organise themselves in terms of a division between deploying jouissance that is phallic and jouissance that is feminine. This does not constitute any kind of bisexuality, because the division is asymmetrical and phallic jouissance is present in both sexes. The fundamental mode of allocation of the subject to just one single sex according to the law has now shifted to allow an allocation to the other sex.

Phallic jouissance supports the subject, through active speech or otherwise, when faced with any anxiety-provoking threat that may be experienced as the will of an Other to have jouissance of them. Even when this phallic jouissance belongs to a woman, it is not of the same order as feminine jouissance. Any individual, man or woman, may easily confuse the two, and yet in no way do they have the same consequences.

Orgasm is an essential organic mode of phallic jouissance, being the culmination of the subject's existence while also experienced as the subject's disappearance. Besides, the fact that orgasm occurs less frequently in women than in men – except in masturbation – means that women have less support from their subjective function here. Formerly, when their phallic jouissance had to be repressed during adolescence in order to satisfy the sexual law, the subject suffered.

Women no longer occupy the position of object of desire to the same extent, and do not present themselves as being 'castrated' to the same degree as before in order to do so, which leads to the fear that they may no longer arouse desire. In phantasy, certainly, masculine desire concerns the woman as phallic object, with the help of imaginary castration, but it is at the moment when the man encounters nothing more than his bodily complement that he finds himself 'fulfilled, and therefore swindled' as Lacan put it. As we have emphasised earlier, when an articulation is achieved between a man's phallic jouissance, which supports him

DOI: 10.4324/9781003285984-8

both as subject and as man, and the supplementary jouissance of a woman, the man acquires the phallus in an entirely different way.

While the equivalence between the phallic and the masculine persists to some degree, notably in the unconscious, phallic jouissance is to a lesser and lesser extent considered to be the exclusive domain of men, since it has become clear that no matter which sex one belongs to, phallic jouissance comes from the achievements of a subject. Because this mode of jouissance is organised around a symbol of masculinity, to call it 'phallic', as psychoanalysis does, may nonetheless be confusing. But it derives from the fact that this symbol is initially constructed as that of the desire of the mother, which the child wants to be in order to satisfy her, before desiring to have it in their turn, in one way or another.

Some women still confuse it with a purely masculine jouissance, and feel they are in a state of imposture or of identification with a man, but nowadays it is more likely to appear to them that it represents the function of subject, which they were deprived of for so long by the very structure of the sexual law. Many women still feel anxious or mistrustful in relation to their specific jouissance; this comes from the fact that, in common with many men, they confuse it with the jouissance of the Other that would abolish them as subject. Whereas in reality, it is a question of what would allow them to have jouissance of the Other as desire and not as object.

It remains true that the necessary passivity, which is also active, that enables the reception of the jouissance of the other, constitutes a form of subjective abandonment that continues to provoke anxiety. It seems that the contemporary suppression of the prohibition of sexual jouissance has entailed the lifting of numerous inhibitions and obstacles, and has opened up a great many possibilities for supplementary jouissance, and yet still at certain points obstacles remain or new ones are being formed. In the majority of cases, however, the feminine mode, deployed in a new way, gives access to subjective jouissance, while preserving feminine jouissance in the 'sexual relation'. We can use a clothing metaphor here in a rather amusing way: while it is now a matter of indifference whether a woman or a man wears the trousers, women have the option of wearing the skirt as a specific modality.

Especially among the younger generations, there seems to be a recognition of the developments that allow a more respectful relation between the sexes, even if doing so lays bare the extent of the gap in that relation. For a man, the access he now has to the woman's jouissance constitutes a pathway to a place outside of a jouissance that is solely phallic, and he may now perceive the latter as being autoerotic, even if it is sanctioned by the law.

II. Sharing of castration

In our century, it has become clear that castration, described by psychoanalysis as a structure that causes anxiety, is omnipresent throughout the world, with no one escaping its effects in their love and sex life, whether it is recognised and overcome, or not. The phallic phase of the infantile unconscious considers castration to be feminine, confusing the phallus with the penis, as in the sexual law, but the development of ideas and social mores has shown that where the sexual act is concerned, it is also on the masculine side as well. Masculinity is coming to be defined differently; it is no longer determined to the same extent by a Father who is exclusively in possession of the phallus, who has command of it in the unconscious, who promulgates the law and who, without limits or castration, makes the mother have jouissance, as that mythical figure gradually disappears from contemporary discourse.

The penis has to a large extent been disentangled from its equivalence with the phallus, and the lack of the phallus is the very meaning of desire. It has become clear that men's search for what it is that is lacking in woman concerns nothing other than the phallus.[1] Castration belongs to each subject of phallic jouissance, whether masculine or feminine, functioning as both its limit and its underpinning. The feminine is less easy to define according to its object, and the female subject is defined more broadly in terms of phallic jouissance.

As the century has progressed, we have resigned ourselves to a number of losses here, and this is especially true among the younger generations. However, psychoanalytic experience continues frequently to show an unconscious amalgam between the penis and the phallus, and thus between the masculine and the phallic. It gives rise to the pathology called penis envy in certain women, and some psychoanalytic notions still see it as something that affects everyone, without grasping the fact that the lack in the woman is above all else wanting to be desired, because that gives her access to her own jouissance. The earliest psychoanalytic ideas concerning the distribution of castration have broadly evolved, since it was once deemed to be entirely on the side of the woman: not having in order to be, and being the object of desire as a value of jouissance. The Lacanian readjustments of sexual theory went alongside massive re-workings of the social bonds between the sexes.

If entering the field of the sexual relation requires one to do so via the phallic function of the law, the actual relation to the other sex, even to sex itself,[2] means going further. Discourse no longer implies that the man *a priori* has the phallus in the name of the Father, nor that the woman is castrated in his name. In the sexual encounter, the sexual law is no longer applied to the same extent as before regarding the roles of the individuals involved, but it is rather a case of sharing being and having between the two partners, at different points. There is no longer a univocal castration of either one or the other; one of them may be phallic in one domain, and the other in another, in such a way as to create a knotting between them.

The phallic dialectic as a whole is far more diverse than it was in the past, far more determined by the articulation of the real jouissances of each party, and far less so by the old sexual law. It still functions partly along the lines of a polarity of more and less, where one of the parties has something as a 'plus' in one register, giving it to the other who has something as a 'minus', and thereby, in the act of giving, being assured that they do indeed possess the 'plus'. This sort of fluctuation or difference of potential between the plus and the minus, obviously relative in relation to each other, is operative in an economy of the sexual relation that now distributes the terms of being and having on a case-by-case basis. But sexuality remains symbolised by things that do not actually concern it, like being and having and the prohibition of incest.

Two possible ways of organising the economy of the sexual couple's relation can be distinguished, on the basis of successive losses of jouissance. Either one party will always subtract more phallic value from the partner, to reach the zero point of castration, or the supplementary gift made to them will come to compensate for the jouissance lost in the sexual relation. The perpetuation of these processes may be achieved through the infinite extension of each stage, especially within the logic of addition or of giving, whereas within the logic of subtraction an obstacle is very soon encountered. The logic of the supplement has a far greater potential for longevity.

The couples formed in our time are far more ephemeral than those formed and sanctioned by the laws of marriage and kinship. The choice made according to inclination, which nowadays has the force of law, is left to itself and endures only as long as its own economy survives, whereas the choice made according to the law of marriage included the third term of the law, imposed in order to keep the two partners in the couple together. There is a widespread notion that the latter system was ruinous in the majority of cases, but this no longer appears to be so certain, if we take into account the economy of the sexual couple left to its own logic, which demonstrates its limitations through the brevity of its survival rate. Nonetheless, it cannot be denied that the union made on the basis of inclination remains a point of progress in civilisation. It means that the apparatus of marriage no longer defines the relation between man and woman, but it remains for us to establish the logics of union that define it.

In this scheme of things, men's anxiety has become more prominent, since women's desire in no longer so silent; the desirable object now becomes the desirer. Even though experience shows that some males are enthusiastic about this type of relation, a man may now find that he feels like an instrument of satisfaction. In other cases, with the evolution of explicit feminine desire, and even sometimes their insistence on having jouissance, it is easy for a confusion to arise with the castrating mother's demand for jouissance. So it may be difficult for a man to overcome this, in order to participate in the other jouissance offered to him by a woman, which would allow him to jettison the law of the mythical Father.

Anxiety remains present for a woman, too, as does castration, because she knows less about what she is in relation to the man's desire once she is no longer reduced by discourse to an object of exchange or marriage. Not being desired is a widespread contemporary form of feminine castration, and her own jouissance, which is now summoned to the table, is neither easily accessible nor easily accepted, by the other or by herself.

So love relations remain marked by the approach of castration anxiety, in the form of the fear of rejection, of abandonment, of 'not being up to it'. Added to this is the fear of losing oneself in the other, of being sucked in by the desire of the other, which generates an anxiety of subjective abolition. Separation sacrifices desire while supporting the subject, because whatever goes in the direction of the realisation of desire often also goes in the direction of the fading of the subject.

In order to compensate for this, everything in the imaginary register that can support the subject and the reconstitution of the ego is deployed, in the phantasy and in the virtual realm, through identification with a model or an image, as is everything that can help to support the subject's fragile desire when faced with that of the Other. Once the desire of the other sex is no longer formalised and kept at a distance by the prohibition of the law, it becomes present without any barrier, for a subject who is ill-equipped to deal with it.

The important role played by masturbation in contemporary discourse is clear here; it is as if the culture of well-being that is regulated by the pleasure principle also resorts to this means, which creates a distance from the jouissance of the Other. Freud commented that the fact that masturbation is unsatisfactory is a fundamental enigma; well, it now seems that it is not as unsatisfactory as all that. It is no longer just a shameful substitute for sexual pleasure that is either absent or avoided, but has become an integral part of various forms of jouissance.

Although the sexual act has not been freed from anxiety through the lifting of prohibition, it is now more open to an authentic experience of jouissance, no longer defined through transgression or submission to the law of discourse. Of course, it still encounters all sorts of inhibitions and excesses, failures and welcome surprises, in diverse and almost infinite forms. But the approach to the other sex or to sex as such now involves the aim of remaining with the other in the field of the 'sexual relation', that of the two of sex, in order to achieve the complex and progressive knotting of one jouissance with another.

III. The 'sexual relation' today

A number of fears that emerge as the prohibition bearing on sexual jouissance disappears are linked to the fact that the prohibition was taken to contribute to the regulation of jouissance, so that if there is no longer any prohibition, some people believe that it will burst forth in an unbridled way. Prohibition is often thought to be the principal support of desire, and indeed this is correct: a certain type of desire is never so intense as when it is forbidden. It is true that prohibition does regulate jouissance and that it arouses desire, but it is not alone in doing so, and it does so only within a limited horizon.

Once the prohibition falls away, desire may sometimes indeed disappear, and may find nothing else to support it; but desire may also be deployed in relation to its attainment, and when confronted with the jouissance that completes it, it is the best defence against whatever this jouissance may involve that is anxiety-provoking. When there is no longer any prohibition, the anxiety caused by the desire of the Other is exposed, as is the difficulty of approaching one's object, and the search begins for the conditions in which desire can be sustained while being articulated with another desire, rather than substituting itself for the latter by repressing it. It is no longer merely a case of winning over the object of desire, but also of managing to articulate one's desire with the other desire and the other jouissance.

In the past, the symbolic structures of kinship were constantly present as a third term between two partners, so that their 'complementary' relation laid down by the law was inscribed within a much wider context. The presence of institutions and ancestral lines made it easier to provide a necessary means of knotting together the desires and the jouissances of each partner in the sexual couple. But now, the bond between the couple is only self-determined, self-authorised, around the imaginary phallic value attributed to each partner, and the hitching together of two unconsciouses in a phantasy. Any possible articulation of two jouissances occurs around the object in the position of third term to which the woman lends herself, rather than the law and lineage. Now that marriages are no longer formed within the family and organised by institutions, and are allowed to form through chance encounters and elective affinities, there are very few symbolic structures to support them. Even the slightest pressure from the paternal system leaves each subject more exposed to the desire of the Other sex, which is a source of desire but also of anxiety. Women's desire is no longer so restricted, and men's desire is no longer sustained by institutions; and in a certain sense it was indeed easier to have to deal with the prohibition rather than the desire of the Other. The construction of a relation of two jouissances within a sexual couple involves a dialectic that is complex in a different way from that of the plus and the minus regulated solely by the phallic function.

The new characteristics of love relations have led to the diminution of a number of elements that are sources of neurosis. Neurotic logic is based entirely on the phallic function, so that in phantasy it remains organised according to the prohibition of the Father, even though the latter no longer has currency in the social bond. Any possible resolution of neurosis resides in giving up that logic, and finding access to another logic in which not everything depends on the phallic function, but neither is it entirely relinquished, and in principle this is favoured by current developments, unless it tips over into discourses of 'all or nothing'.

As the type of relation created on the basis of sexual law tends to be fading, analytic experience is seeing the disappearance of the difficulties it once engendered, while at the same time other difficulties are appearing, which show a certain structural continuity. The 'complementary' mode of relation established between a subject and their object is so fundamental that when this condition is no longer satisfied between a man and a woman according to the sexual law, it becomes displaced and emerges elsewhere: towards a child, the same sex, or a virtual or toxic jouissance, and there are other possibilities too. So now, the framework of each encounter in the field of love explicitly involves the attempt to knot together two desires, while purely sexual encounters concern nothing other than the object of desire. Obviously this was the case in the past, too, but only one desire was 'legitimised', and the repression of that of the other was required by discourse.

Nonetheless, the separation of love and sexual desire still occurs frequently, while the prohibition of sexual jouissance has disappeared, and the prohibition of incest no longer extends beyond its own field. This is a striking observation, and has weighty consequences. We still find on a regular basis that some people cannot love the one who is desired, or cannot desire the one who is loved. This remains a fundamental division, at play between the two sexes, as if the contamination of incest inherent in all sexual desire persists, and no solution can be found.

The different modes of women's jouissance, between what a woman is for a man and what she is in herself as subject, are now quite clear, and this division is openly recognised. The man, too, finds himself confronted with a division in a new way, since he has had to give up the castration he formerly sought in the woman, so that once he has achieved this, he may then approach the other jouissance that conjugates the two of sex. He may also not do so, and may have recourse to other modes of castration as a condition of the sexual encounter, but if he can manage to accept the loss, he will be in a position to approach the other jouissance with a woman.

Nowadays, engaging with the other in sexual terms without the paternal system of prohibition and the law of exchange is the norm in our society. What is at stake is the knotting of two modes of jouissance rather than eliding one of the two. Far more often than in the past, the desire of a woman is the determining factor in the establishment of a love relation, and is no longer something that circulates only in the interstices of discourse. However, the inhibition and the prohibition that some women inflict upon themselves remain present, while, on the contrary, some develop a form of bulimia with love and sex, which was once a characteristic of men.

The desire of women does not produce a universal discourse. It is either supported by a phallic jouissance of the subject, in which case it is not feminine but neuter, or else it is supported by a feminine jouissance, and in that case it circulates outside discourse. Its medium is a saying rather than a statement, just as it was in the past, since the two cannot be articulated in discourse. The new way of relating to the other sex is characterised by the fact that nothing has been decided that would be valid for everyone; each sexual couple invents and constructs its own way, without constituting a discourse or a rule for all.

These days we encounter all sorts of variations in the approach to the other sex, even if the terms of the old sexual law are still present and constitute an essential reference. A significant number of couples are still formed on the basis of a circulation of the phallus that obeys the sexual law: 'he has it, she is it'. And a number of women, while they subscribe to this, do not simply remain in that position, but develop a supplementary jouissance, which exists without ever being inscribed anywhere. Or else a relation is formed with the help of another type of object that allows two desires to be knotted together through its function as intermediary. Or again, a number of couples are formed by developing a fraternal relation, from which jouissance is more or less excluded. Often, an attempted relation will fail if each party adopts a position that mirrors that of the other, where both situate themselves either as object or as subject; in such cases of equivalence, no relation can be produced.

Whatever the choice may be that organises the relation, it can be resolved only within this framework. There are an enormous number of diverse possibilities of articulation in the heterosexual couple, as well as in homosexuality or in the 'perversions' that are now known as 'sexual variations'. Contemporary sexual minorities are engaged in laying claim to a great number of denominations of their modes of jouissance in order to form the basis of their social identities. Some are moving toward the construction of a relation on the basis of the not-all-phallic, others are reverting to the complementary mode according to the all-phallic, but in ways that are different from those that failed in the past.

Yet such an immense upheaval could not occur without some problematic effects. Certain discourses openly evince their nostalgia for the old system and their rejection of the new. Among the causes of the re-emergence of violent religious movements, the development of the relation between the sexes in the Western world associated with the fading of belief in the Christian God has certainly played a significant role. On the other hand, some equally radical discourses preach the eradication of the 'old patriarchal systems' and the whole framework of phallic logic, and even a complete suppression of models of masculinity and femininity, proclaiming a total independence in the choice of sexuated identity in relation to anatomical sex. Furthermore, a number of sexual minorities refuse the term 'choice' to designate sexual orientation. If, indeed, it is a choice, then it is an unconscious one, so therefore involuntary and generally impossible to modify. So they feel that it is not a choice at all, in the sense that it is currently understood, but rather a destiny that is imposed on them. That is understandable; however, recognising the unconscious choice as one's own has significant psychical effects, even though this may result in a reduction in its role in activism.

Psychoanalysis has shown how a logic of the not-all-phallic has become an adjunct to the phallic logic of patriarchal societies, and it has described the wellsprings and the functioning of the former, while studying the ways in which our discourses can manage without the prototype of the Father, while still making use of it. Our structures do not require that different functions must all be appropriated by one single paternal agency, but they nevertheless need to ensure that those functions are still carried out by other, diverse agencies.

IV. Masculinity unlocked

One of the significant questions raised by these developments concerns that status of the masculine position. The reduction of belief in the Father's function has had the effect of unlocking the masculine from being determined by the paternal, and loosening the boundaries of the enclosed space of the 'all' that he had contributed to creating. In the past, being determined by the phallic function linked to the mythical Father, a man had no choice other than submission or identification. From this arose the obsession with the murder of the Father and with seizing his objects of desire. The Oedipal enclave, which used to function universally, is now only regional. The impact of the receding of the law has had far-reaching effects on the masculine just as much as on the feminine, since each is defined in relation to the other.

It might seem unthinkable that a conjunction of jouissances facilitated by the intervention of supplementary jouissance can be possible which does not annul the man's phallic desire and jouissance but actually requires it. It is indeed difficult to imagine this against the background of the phallic function, based on one jouissance alone, and so in one sense none at all. And it would be difficult not to attribute the same principle of an autoerotic relation of subject to object, to the other sex. The inhibition or disappearance of desire may gain the upper hand, or indeed the converse may occur in the form of a radicalisation of the sexual relation according to phallic jouissance alone, in a way that may become bulimic or addictive.

The 'debasement' described by Freud in terms of the impossibility of desiring a woman who is loved or of loving a woman who is desired, continues to be present as our society evolves and even finds new arguments in its favour. One example of Freud's 'debasement' is to love the woman who is desired only long enough to ensure that she is possessed, and then to disinvest the relation. This splitting of love and desire manifestly represents a powerful mode of defence against the anxiety surrounding incest, which is paradoxically amplified once the prohibition of incest has been reduced to its concrete meaning, because the Father is no longer there to intervene.

There are all kinds of diversions, dodges, ruptures and progressive adjustments involved in approaching the possibility of a real 'sexual relation'. One man, for example, may hold on to the traditional phallic position within a couple, and may at the same time knot together a relation in which he is the one who is desired. Another may enter into multiple loveless relations, in an identification with the mythical Father, having failed in a relation in which the aim was to knot two jouissances together. Certainly, these types of impossibility and the solutions found to them are far from being new, but they take on new forms in the way they occur within a framework where the phallic organisation of the relation between the sexes according to the law is only present in a discreet, or even silent, way, and is, it seems, merely contingent.

V. Feminine, plural

It has now become clear that the feminine can be divided into two specific modes of jouissance. The far-reaching reorganisation of this field includes the possibility of deploying a specifically feminine jouissance just as much as a phallic jouissance of the subject, which was previously absorbed into inhibition or simply into motherhood.

The jouissance that is called supplementary, which involves receiving one's jouissance from the Other, while lending oneself to being the object of desire while also deploying one's own desire, can only come into being through giving up the function of the mythical Father, while still partially satisfying the phallic function. It is the mode *par excellence* of the logic of the 'not-all', which requires a subjective dynamic shift outside neurosis. The castration at stake is in one way that of the woman, and in another that of the man. What enables the knotting within the sexual couple is the imaginary gift of the woman, whereas the one-way circulation of the phallus formed a knot only in creating a hierarchical chain with the agency of the Father. Certainly, what once went without saying, in silence in a speechless discourse, is now put into words.

This field is also open to those women who choose to give up on this jouissance, who are only able to desire a man they do not love, or love a man they do not desire. In such cases, the man who is loved is somehow forbidden sexually, as if combining the two aspects had an incestuous dimension; this may happen when a father or a brother remain over-invested, and the love for him extends its prohibition to every man who inspires love in the woman. In these cases, too, we find a neurotic logic of the 'all', poorly demarcating the borderline of the prohibition of incest in the unconscious, alongside a difficulty in bringing together the affectionate and sensual currents once they have been separated at the point of emergence from the Oedipus complex. The persistence of this splitting, at a time when the prohibition of incest no longer goes beyond its own borders, suggests that the incestuous phantasy is both the cause of the splitting and what is called upon to come to the rescue when one is faced with the discovery of the sexual non-relation. Indeed, it forms an exception, in that it is a sexual relation that would reunite the two currents.[3]

Another way of blocking access to the 'sexual relation' with a man who is loved is to love a man who does not respond to this love, and in such cases the love may survive for a long time, without coming to grief on the impossibility of passage to the sexual act. Or a woman may make a host of demands on a man at the first sign of his desire, in order to impose a phantasy of man onto him, without taking account of the reality of this partner, and this generally results in the disappearance of his desire. In such cases, everything happens as if the absence of the man's desire were ultimately more bearable, even though as soon as there is a sign of it, she gives herself over to him completely.

All sorts of symptoms aim to block access to the sexual relation, now that it is no longer subject to prohibition. There are bulimic modes of jouissance that may involve participation in an identification with the object of jouissance of the mythical Father, or even in a phallic jouissance deployed in the masculine way. A number of women, having succeeded brilliantly in whatever mattered to them in the professional domain, may conversely adopt a radically passive attitude in the field of love, expecting everything to come from the man, and may orientate themselves entirely according to the phallic function of the sexual law. When their phallic jouissance is satisfied within their professional framework, they conversely identify totally with the object of desire in the sexual relation. In certain literary genres we can observe a frisson of masochistic phantasy, where on the basis of a contract, a man plays the role of executioner, at a time when the law no longer designates him as the master.

Other styles of relation give up on sexual jouissance, displacing it onto what consists in having the other at one's disposal. Having jouissance of the 'possession' of a man suffices in such cases, rather than having jouissance with him, and this may be achieved through living with him. Making oneself the metaphor of the jouissance of the man requires that one should not have jouissance; some women, for example, consider that by living with him, they have given themself to him, and so cannot give him their jouissance as well. It has always been the case that this metaphorical mode of jouissance can easily takes over, once sexual desire has disappeared through cohabitation or the birth of children. It is easy to see how this symbolic form of jouissance has always been compatible with the sexual law, consisting as it does in the continued presence of the other and the representation of the bond between them, and where sexual desire is left entirely to the man, as if it concerned him alone.

Some women give themselves up entirely to the desire of the other when they enter a couple; their own desire disappears, and only reappears when the relation breaks up, which severely affects their chances of living as a couple. After repeated failures, they may find stability in a fruitful and active solitude, and may even have ephemeral relations, finding it hard to admit to themselves that they like it that way, or they may have numerous virtual encounters. Choosing a man who in their eyes has no phallus, whether in social, cultural or racial terms, allows them to respond to certain impasses, and may suit nicely the fact that things are also inverted at the level of sexual jouissance. A different sharing of phallic distribution, between discourse and jouissance, allows them to be knotted together.

Psychoanalysis generally favours the passage to another logic beyond the all-phallic, whether it is that of femininity, creative sublimation or even that of becoming an analyst. It facilitates access to a real 'sexual relation', and opens up a pathway out of neurosis.

VI. Love as suppleance

Nowadays it is broadly accepted that love is not always a necessary adjunct to sex, for women or for men. Even if love is sought and desired, and the bonds that comprise it are privileged, a large part of sexual life unfolds without love, or includes only a brief period of love. The separation between sex and love takes a number of different forms, showing that it has a structural dimension that goes beyond individual cases.

Love, however, remains the most widespread and the most effective suppleance to the absence of the sexual relation, especially the feminine love that establishes the supplementary mode of jouissance, not accepting the deficiency of the sexual act but rather adding something to it. How can we conceive of love being a suppleance to the failed 'sexual relation' when it appears to be the relation itself? The fact that modernity called upon love to be the foundation of marriage, while clearly constituting progress in a way, has something of pathos about it, since love is precisely what comes into being when it fails. In some way, this type of relation consists in basing a bond on what covers over the gap that the relation itself involves.

Love often occurs in the feminine mode of jouissance, at the point where, from being the one who is loved, the woman become the one who loves, and this substitution is the well-spring of supplementary jouissance.[4] We know, however, that being loved can also lead to loving . . . someone else. Which means it is no longer a metaphor of love, but a metonymy fleeing from desire, and which instead of creating a reversal towards the one who loves, produces a displacement from them towards someone else. This does not represent a feminine jouissance at all, but rather a mode of carrying forward phallic jouissance to another place, following the phallic model. This difference is palpable, in love, between a metaphorical process of substitution, where the lover is substituted for the loved one, establishing a supplementary jouissance that identifies the lack and supplements it, and a process of metonymic displacement, which carries the jouissance as value into a different place, in order to negate lack.

The division between love without desire and desire without love constitutes the displacement that is established at the same crossroads of the sexual act, where supplementary jouissance responds with its metaphor. Where one will carry forward the subtracted jouissance, the other refuses subtraction and supplements it by responding to the lover with jouissance and love. Love implies a knowledge of castration, that of the other as well as one's own, and the idealisation that it consists of is constructed precisely on the repressed knowledge of this lack.

These processes can be found in both women and men, which deal with the disjunction of jouissances in different ways, with very distinct effects. Masculine logic is more likely to involve the metonymic mode of carrying over phallic jouissance, annulling and repressing the non-relation. Feminine logic, where it has been established, involves a metaphorical mode of inversion that does not annul lack but adds something to it. This is why for a man, feminine jouissance constitutes the 'moment of truth', and he may either evade it or, on the contrary, partake in it. By having a different relation with two women, according to the process of carrying forward, a man may believe that he has a relation with the woman as defined by the phallic function. The reversal of love onto the Other produces something different, and it is in such cases that we may speak of suppleance through love.

The process of love is linked to a subjective inversion, to a change of discourse. It shares with the creative act this same subjective position, consisting in identifying a lack and supplementing it bit by bit, piece by piece, through successive adjustments, like a love without object or love of a work. This elaboration in itself constitutes a jouissance. This is one of the reasons why it was thought for a long time that if a woman brought this form of jouissance into being, it entailed the renunciation of sexual jouissance, whereas in fact case love and sexual jouissance are linked here.

What the sexual act reveals as a lack of relation and as castration for both part-ners may cause a reversal on the basis of which suppleances can be created. In such cases it does not cause love to wither away, but rather increases it. Love as such is not sexuated, even if jouissance is; it aims at the Other to whom demand is addressed before the Other is included as sexed. It concerns the Other as the fundamental partner in language, the one who at the time of the resolution of the Oedipus complex was emptied of jouissance in order to facilitate the formation of the subject.

So when love emerges, it consists in replenishing this space that has been emp-tied out, with jouissance. It rejects the emptying out of jouissance from the Other, which is also that of the subject. It is a sort of foreclosure of the emptiness of the Other that allows it to be replenished with a jouissance, and in this process love causes 'madness'. In supplementary jouissance, love rejects the lack in the 'sexual relation' and aims to supplement it, recognising the truth of the but not submit-ting to it; it does not obliterate the lack, but it overcomes the obstacle. Phallic jouissance proceeds quite differently, since it also refuses the lack, but in a way that annuls it, represses it and simply takes the subtracted value somewhere else, carrying it forward.

Throughout the ages, the civilised couple was defined according to a whole gamut of prescriptions and prohibitions that organised the framework in which sexuality was inscribed, not so much because the law shaped desire, but rather because the unconscious desire of the phallic function shaped the law. Freud and the first psychoanalysts created a stark picture of what sexuality consisted of within this framework, in terms of symptoms, blind alleys and obstacles. Of course, this did not exclude sexualities that worked well and happily, in propor-tions impossible to determine, since they were the ones that did not find their way into the psychoanalyst's consulting room. Since the 1970s, this framework and its prohibitions have more or less disappeared from discourses and readjustments have been made in psychoanalytic thinking through Lacan's work, and now that of his students. Our search for clarity requires us to recognise the advantages and disadvantages of any system, so that the question for psychoanalysis, with the current developments in our society, is to give the most logical account possible of what the new situation offers in comparison to the old one.

We live in an era when the laws determining social bonds have ceased to fix the roles of each sex and their sexual objects, leaving them to the whim of each subject and each couple; and anatomical sex constitutes one attribute among oth-ers, but is no longer a destiny. The upheaval that this constitutes, whether on a small or large scale, at the level of subjectivity, or of politics and religion, is considerable. What is more, the law of most Western countries has extended the right of marriage to all couples, including homosexuals, in order to extend neces-sary rights to sexual minorities, whereas for millennia it had insisted on the union of the two sexes. Recognising the lack of their articulation in a relation, the law inscribed one in the heart of the same, so that what it takes to form a couple could be deployed there, too.

The picture of the couple drawn by Freud at the start of the last century continues to show us just how accurately he pinpointed the impasses of sexual jouissance at the time when it was subject to prohibition. Although he quite rightly referred the 'debasement in the field of love' to the anxiety about incest evoked by the love object, the continuation of the separation between sex and love calls for another reading of the function of prohibition.[5] Now that the function of the Father as model has been deconstructed, it does not mean that anxiety has been diminished; quite the contrary, since he imposed a law that enabled a distance to be kept from maternal incest, even if this meant a certain paternal incest.

The dwindling belief in the Father in the discourses of the Western world has allowed a degree of loosening of the chains he imposed, including the universality of the sexual law, so that it has become apparent that the law was not based on a relation between two sexes, and that sex is not the basis of a relation that can be inscribed. We may think, then, that the law was a modality of inscription at one given stage in the history of our civilisation, which allowed the problematic concept of the relation between the sexes to be delegated to the eternal Father. The sexual jouissance that was excluded by the law is now prominent in discourse, and has revealed its own lack.

No other discourse has emerged that tries to establish a new universal conception of the 'sexual relation'. A relation without universality has been unveiled, which leaves each individual to the law of contingency, to the particular, to the unary. It is certainly striking that something as crucial and as essential as the relation to the other sex, and to sex itself, however intimate, should be left to the liberty and the responsibility, the aptitude or ineptitude, of each individual, after being left to 'God's sexual ineptitude'[6] for so very long.

Notes

1 See Lacan, *Anxiety*, op. cit., p. 199.
2 While I have restricted this study to heterosexual relations, it is important to emphasise that a large number of the reflections gathered together here are equally valid for homosexual relations.
3 This thesis was explored in my 'Le moment adolescent', a paper given at the Journées d'Espace analytique, *L'événement adolescent au regard de la psychanalyse*, 5 and 6 December 2015, Paris, published in *Figures de la psychanalyse*, No. 33, Toulouse, Érès, 2017.
4 What Lacan called the metaphor of love, and which he first described in the Platonic pair of *erastes* and *eromenos*; Lacan, *Transference, The Seminar of Jacques Lacan, Book 8*, ed. J-A Miller, Cambridge, Polity, 2015.
5 See my 'Partition du sexe et de l'amour', *Figures de la psychanalyse*, No. 23, Toulouse, Érès, 2012.
6 See Jacques Derrida, *Artaud le Moma*, Paris, Galilée, 2002.

Conclusion

In 2004, my research concluded with a hypothesis, in the conditional mode, leaving space for evidence, in the form of what is happening around us today. Let us summarise the main ideas.

The century of so-called sexual liberation had a profound effect on established ideologies, reducing them to ashes in the hope of finding the possibility of an intact sexual jouissance glowing in their embers. But is that possible? When prohibition disappears, jouissance comes up against an obstacle that limits it in a different way. An impossibility is revealed, and along with that, a completely different logic. An unexpected real flashed out fleetingly, and then more and more insistently as the old symbols were undone. It is indeed strange to think that the relation between man and woman established by discourse was constructed on the basis of an interpretation of their sexual relation. To think that the sexual act, silenced by prohibition, excluded from everything that regulated our symbolic order, nonetheless concealed a central cause. What binds man and woman, in their sexual embrace, suffers from a gap that derives from the sexual law that governed them for so long, but also from another kind of gap that has always existed. Traditional logic found such twisted thinking repellent. It wanted to believe that a cause is a cause and does not change places with its effect. The way the sexual relation is dealt with in civilisation must surely depend on the discourses that civilisations establish; it cannot be that those discourses depend on the sexual relation. Such a hypothesis would be impossible to imagine.

And yet the history of civilisations displays traces of this: in ancient China, for example, the man was exhorted to wilfully postpone the final termination of the sexual act. A civilisation, in its myths, would accentuate the means of obtaining jouissance in copulation rather than the procreation that it served to bring about. Nature does not intend it to be like this, offering jouissance in the process of fertilisation rather than copulating in order to have jouissance, preoccupied not with jouissances that are conjoined but only with the arrival of the seed at its destination. Christianity espoused the cause of nature, opting for fertility over jouissance, and taking the metaphor from Genesis as the basis of our sexual law. There, the God of the Bible was responsible for the subtraction of a body part, just as the erection is subtracted, putting an end to the sexual act the moment the semen has been released.

DOI: 10.4324/9781003285984-9

The phallus no longer aimed to ensure jouissance, but only fertility, and through this the disjunction of two jouissances became eternal. The law required one of the parties to have jouissance – however little – in having the body of another at their disposal, while the other only represented this jouissance. The one thought he had jouissance of the other's body, and as for the other – nobody knew.

The unconscious works in the same way, on the basis of incestuous desire prohibited in childhood, in order to construct access later on to the sexual relation. Prohibiting the mother in some sense involves the prescription of initially desiring her, before substituting another object for her that is without desire, as is the case with the sexual law. There, too, phallic regulation is the domain of the Father, who orders castration, from which the relation of man and woman is derived, and there, too, we find a lack of conjunction of their desires and jouissances. When the law of the Father recedes, incestuous desire comes to haunt the sexual act with greater intensity.

But this alone does not constitute the stumbling block. The more overtly a lack is shown to separate the jouissance of one from that of the other, the more the law exiles them from each other, the more their desires vacillate when faced with the castration that results from this, and the more insistently a nostalgia for the mythical union with the mother or father emerges. And the more the pathway to a relation becomes blocked, through prohibition and anxiety. To the point where we may think that the lack of sexual union, the impossibility of the articulation of two jouissances in discourse, generates incest as the myth of a union without a lack, even though it is prohibited. In that case, the two could become One, the sexual relation would exist if it was allowed. It exists in this way through its very prohibition: the incestuous myths of ancient Greece had represented this, as, it seems, had Sophocles.

The relation between the sexes has suffered from the sexual law, which itself was based on the cut encountered in every single sexual relation as its natural ending, as its eternal commandment. Incarnating the limit of pleasure, whether it has gone well or not, it separates the couple and extracts the instrument of jouissance just as God extracted the rib. For the man, it creates an imaginary Eve, an ideal value carried forward from the organ that has been subtracted. Having this value, or being it for the other, is the basis of the law between the sexes. Their jouissances can never be conjoined, other than occasionally outside discourse.

The sexual law is no longer universal in the Western world, as it once was, but is one possibility among others; it is no longer the reference of the law that is imposed, but a reference taken from the imaginary that desires. Psychoanalytic experience has uncovered the absence that is revealed once it no longer determines the law, when it shows itself to be a fiction, having once been deemed a universal truth. There is still nothing within a discourse that allows the desire and the jouissance of one sex to be articulated with that of the other, and this may turn out to be the very impossibility that our century of the deconstruction of the Father has discovered, once it is no longer blinded by prohibition, and as it takes the measure of its twist and turns. What's left is the chance of a jouissance that makes itself an exception to the law, while still accepting it partially. It may manage to unite a particular couple, and do the same for others too. Such jouissance is not always, like Eurydice, lost twice over.

***

At the time of publication, 18 years after the work was completed, the facts seem to confirm my hypothesis. In the last century, Freud inaugurated a new kind of knowledge about sex, through his deciphering of the effects of the prohibition of incest in the unconscious. The birth of psychoanalysis threw light on the discourses that had been passed down to us through the philosophy and mythology of ancient Greece, its alphabet and its grammar, Oedipus and the phallic symbolic, creating the basis of the power of the logos. It lifted a corner of the veil that had been drawn over sex throughout history, having expelled it from discourse in our Western Christian civilisation. But at that time, psychoanalysis did not enlighten us about the facts of the sexual relation. There was nothing in it that enabled us to understand why the East had come up with something entirely different regarding sex from the law of incest, and especially the conditions for jouissance. The points of correspondence between the unconscious knowledge of modern man and the traditions of ancient sexual knowledge did not enable us to locate the point at which they were joined together.

In order to do that, we needed to explore the whole range of Lacan's discoveries about the 'sexual relation', developing what Freud had suspected. All it took was to describe our sexual encounters from the point of view of their most immediate, most intimate aspect, which is completely obvious but was never spoken about, and the way it took place between man and woman, in its absolutely constant trajectory. He just had to point out that it is the psychical law of pleasure, as an unconscious, subjective regulation of the sexual act, that puts an end to it, for both parties, whether satisfying or not, leaving the conjunction of jouissances indeterminate. Here, however, we had the most obvious – and the almost unnoticed – occurrence of the biological 'rock' whose existence Freud, quite remarkably, had suspected, as he struggled in his latter years to try to understand what essential biological law had given such strength and power in the unconscious to what he had called the castration complex. The way masculine subjectivity was knotted with the scansion of jouissance supplied discourse with a grammar. This borrowing from phallic jouissance, eliding the other jouissance, formed the pivot of a sexual law within the institutions of language, substituting the 1 and its object for the two of sex, while distributing the functions of discourse between them.

In addition to the hole excavated in our symbolic order by the prohibition of incest, we also have this gap in the 'sexual relation'. These are the two great causes operative in the unconscious. Incestuous desire leaves its traces in subjectivity, because it is formed on the basis of the simple logic that follows from the fact that humans beings speak, are born of the woman who carries them, and receive the Law in one form or another. The gap in the 'sexual relation' has consequently produced a grammar that constructs a discourse without 'two'. Instead of allowing the disjointed jouissances to be knotted in threes, monotheism effected a cut between them, and constructed nothing other than the One alone with his complement.

The veil is lifted when these constructions fall apart, and when functions that are necessary are redistributed in a different way. In our time, while the Father of the unconscious continues to hold sway to some extent, the logos no longer insists on privileging procreation; subjectivity is allowed to regulate its own jouissance. Admitting the difficulty of constructing the two of sex, our societies have opened up pathways which may allow it to be possible. Without appealing to nature where the sexual relation is concerned, the current way of thinking is closer to it, since jouissance has been restored alongside fertility, and femininity alongside masculinity. And, refusing to accept that one law should proscribe to everyone what this relation should be, we are left free – and alone – to determine what it might be, this relation that is not, after all, universal.

Index